The NEW
Better
Behavior
In Dogs

The NEW
Better
Behavior
In Dogs
A Guide to Solving All Your Dog Problems

William E. Campbell
Illustrated by Robert M. Miller

Alpine

PUBLICATIONS

Alpine Publications, Inc., Loveland, Colorado

*The New Better Behavior in Dogs: A Guide to Solving
All Your Dog's Problems*

ISBN 1-57779-018-9

Library of Congress Cataloging-in-Publication Data

Campbell, William E. (William Edward). 1929-
    Better behavior in dogs : a guide to solving all your dog problems
    William E. Campbell : illustrated by Robert M. Miller.
      p. cm.
    Rev. ed. of: Owner's guide to better behavior in dogs. 2nd ed.
c 1995.
    Includes bibliographical references (p.)
    ISBN 1-57779-018-9
    1. Dogs--Behavior. 2. Dogs--Training. I. Campbell, William E.
(William Edward), 1929- Owner's guide to better behavior in dogs.
II. Title. III. Title: Better behavior in dogs.
SF433.C9525 1999   99-10974
636.7 ' 088 ' 7--DC21   CIP

Cover Photo by Faith Uridel. Ch. Winterwheat's Illusive Glance,
   ("Jamie") Number 1 Soft Coated Wheaten bitch in 1991 and 1992.
Illustrations by Robert M. Miller, DVM.
Cover Design: Bob Schram

    3 4 5 6 7 8 9 0

Printed in the United States of America.

TABLE OF CONTENTS

PART IV   WHEN YOU NEED MORE HELP

Acknowledgments

Dare Miller, who introduced me to this field and pioneered the causative approach to behavior problems in dogs.

The University of California, Los Angeles biomedical library for making available all the United States and foreign research literature which was to be the knowledge base for so many practical concepts.

The late Herbert Snow, DVM, whose invitation to lecture at UCLA forced me to formalize my ideas.

Fred Smithcors, DVM, Ph.D., who made me contributing editor to *Modern Veterinary Practice* magazine in 1972 and published the first edition of *Behavior Problems in Dogs*.

Betty Jo McKinney, publisher, Alpine Publications, for seeing the value of a third revised edition of this book.

John P. Scott and the late John L. Fuller for your tireless work and selfless sharing of ideas in *Dog Behavior, The Genetic Basis*.

Michael Fox, veterinarian who provided the spark that kindled behavioral interest among veterinarians in the 1960s.

Jack and Wendy Volhard, the deans of obedience instruction, who adapted to that world my behavioral test for selecting puppies.

Special thanks to Tally, our Dalmatian, Randy, our Norwegian Elkhound, and Punkin, our Miniature Dachshund, family members and indispensable colleagues on our behavioral team, providing living examples for the ideal: To be in the world, but not of it; free from ambition, greed, intellectual pride, blind obedience to custom, or awe of those higher in rank; understanding that an attitude, like a virtue or a vice, cannot be taught, it must be "caught."

Thanks: Robert M. Miller, DVM, "RMM." Your genius brings to our visual senses, with humor, the essence of ideas that defy verbal description.

Finally, to my wife, Peggy. Words cannot describe her contribution.

Foreword

Better Behavior in Dogs is an invaluable tool for solving behavior problems and training. It's the only book I will use for my students.

There are giants and pioneers in every field. In the field of animal behavior and training, Bill Campbell is just that! He is the steady force behind a growing movement that embraces a philosophy based on humane and ethic practices. The "Learn to Earn or No Free Lunch Program" and "Orienting Reflex Techniques" are instruction methods established by Bill in the 1970s. These easily learned skills have been used and adapted by many professionals in our field. Bill's methods reveal that every relationship between dog and owner is unique. In my experience, no one knows dogs better and with such compassion. He also understands dogs' roles in families and how emotions and activities within families affect dogs.

When I was new in this field, I was dismayed by the prevalent indifference of animal behavior professionals toward animals as feeling creatures. The dignity of these creatures was often dismissed by the employment of inhumane training and products. Sadly, there is a lot of money to be made in the dog business, often at the expense of dogs and their owners. The inundation of information and the myriad of quick fixes, combined with an ever-increasing fast pace of life, puts inexperienced dog owners at a perilous disadvantage.

"You cannot go to the next step until you are comfortable and in control of your dog's emotions. Solving behavior problems and training is an integrated process," Bill says. "Dog and owner as team must move at their own pace." *Better Behavior in Dogs* is a direct, practical guide for the beginner and the professional; and one to be used as a reference indefinitely. This book belongs in the library of every dog lover. Reading it is a pleasure, as are RMM's delightful illustrations. Are you and your dog on the "Alpha See-Saw?" Are you experiencing those "Alpha Pulls" on dog walks? Read this book. You'll both be better for it!

Gleanna Doyle,
Dog Behavior Training Specialist; Founder, My Dog's Place

Introduction

The symbiotic relationship between man and dog goes back to the earliest phases of mankind's development. Both creatures were hunters. Both lived in small groups—a band or pack—and both were governed by a complex social order. Both species lived by their wits, lacking the physical power of the great predators such as the lion and sabre-toothed tiger, and used strategy and the strength of numbers to bring home game. The puppy fit into the primitive cave domicile, serving as a playmate for human children, an entertaining companion for the adults, and was the source and recipient of affection and stroking. The dog's keener senses were invaluable to man in guarding his territory, and in locating, pursuing and bringing down game. Much later, when man became a pastoral nomad, the dog herded his flocks. The fact that man often abused the dog, and sometimes ate him, doesn't alter the intensely close relationship between the two species. Thus, man and dog have an extremely long and traditional relationship. Most people instinctively like dogs. Watch a toddler as a friendly dog approaches. Observe people of all ages as they crowd up to the pet shop window. The dog is historically secure in this place as man's best friend.

The sciences of human psychology and human behavior are a mere century old. The sciences of animal behavior and ethology (comparative behavior) are much younger. We are only beginning to understand that each species inherits behavioral characteristics peculiar to it, which helped that species to survive and develop in a hostile environment. There are many differences between the inherent behavioral characteristics of man and dog. Our imprinting and learning patterns differ. We signal aggression, submission, territorial possession, the desire to play, and the desire to mate in very different ways. Yet, as we shall see in Bill Campbell's excellent and perceptive book, there are many similarities between our behavior and that of our canine friends.

Campbell's techniques go beyond the usual dog training rote and often fallacious methods. He examines, understands, and uses the dog's inherent responses to produce a well-adjusted dog. One of life's greatest pleasure, indeed, is a mannerly and well-adjusted dog. Most of us know that and crave such a relationship. Too often, however, things don't go as we had hoped, and it can be a great problem, a stress, a liability, and even a danger. This book brings to the average literate dog owner an understanding of basic canine behavior, together with techniques to produce a well-mannered and happy dog.

R. M. Miller, DVM
Thousand Oaks, California

Preface

If you're like most people, you don't want to inflict pain or emotional stress on your dog: All you really want is come, sit and stay when told, and otherwise stay out of trouble. You don't want your dog to chew up your shoes, poop or pee in the house, jump on guests, bite the mailman, or run into the street and get killed or cause an accident. If you have raised a dog before, you know that achieving this kind of behavior from a normal puppy or older dog isn't automatic. Pups chew in order to teethe or taste things, just like human babies. They have to be taught where (and when) to go to the bathroom, like babies. They love to run around and jump to develop their motor skills, like kids. When they become canine teenagers (at about six months) they feel a need to perform some sort of work as a member of their "pack," like barking at visitors or noises from outside their territory.

During all phases of personality and behavioral development, the way we treat our pups shapes their future behavior and the quality of our relationship with them. Fortunately, most people have only minor problems. But not me. I have always had more difficulty than most, which is probably why I've loved counseling and suffering with thousands of dog owners referred by their veterinarians for thirty-one years. I feel with people who have dog problems. I also feel for their troublesome pets. They aren't trying to be bad. They're just releasing pent-up tensions created by the frustration of living with well-meaning people who usually don't understand them. In virtually all cases of dog behavior problems, that's the truth. I know, because I've been there.

I was devastated as a six-year-old when our little Poodle got out the front door and was run over by a car. We had never taught him to stay out of the street. My teens were spent with a little mixed breed we called a "toy Collie." At first, Dad locked him in the kitchen at night. When Sandy messed on the floor, he'd get his nose stuck into the stuff, his rump swatted and his body rudely "booted" out to the back yard. When he scratched the door at night, Dad would jump out of bed, burst into the kitchen, and whale the tar out of him. The yowling was pitiful. Pretty soon, Sandy started growling at Dad in the morning at the kitchen door. He really got a whuppin' for that.

xi

After a month of this escalating abuse, I stayed awake until the folks went to bed, sneaked to the kitchen and carried Sandy back to my bedroom. To my amazement, he slept all night and woke me just before the folks' alarm went off! I then smuggled him back to the kitchen. Dad was delighted when he opened the door. There was no mess, and he'd enjoyed a great night's sleep. Just how Sandy knew what time to wake me was a mystery then. The way I figure it, Sandy's "time-smarts" saved the relationship between Dad and him.

After a stint in the army in the mid-forties and GI Bill schooling in communications arts, I got a mixed Springer Spaniel puppy. He was supposed to be Cocker size. Ami wound up big as a Labrador Retriever and was literally "wound-up." He couldn't stay still unless asleep. He could jump a five-foot fence and run thirty-seven miles an hour. He beat me to work at the radio station every day. During a weekend outing in the Idaho mountains, he was last seen disappearing over a distant mountain top, hot on the trail of a buck deer. I was crushed, and searched vainly for several weekends. Then a logger described a mill mascot. It was Ami. The logger said Ami seemed happy with his new home and his new name, "Scout." A sage once said, "If you want to find out if your dog is really 'yours,' give him his freedom." I figured he was better off and went home, a thoroughly disillusioned ex-dog owner.

Fifteen years later, after a seven-year career teaching employee motivation with an international company, I returned to Los Angeles, frustrated by the politics of corporate life. Steeped in the psychology of human behavior, I was ready for independence, with an opportunity to continue counseling and making life more rewarding for people. That's when the chance occurred to work with Dare Miller, Ph.D., founder of the Canine Behavior Center in west Los Angeles. His valuable guidance regarding training and the dog-owner relationship merged well with my background in counseling people toward new attitudes. Four years later, Peggy, our four-year-old Dalmatian, Tally, and I (the kids were out on their own) founded the Dog Owner Guidance Services at our Sun Valley Ranch.

I spent seven days a week consulting with dog owners, and countless evenings studying priceless knowledge about dogs and humans from the world's richest source, UCLA's biomedical and psychology libraries. For instance, Sandy's uncanny ability to predict Dad's alarm clock was explained by brain-wave research from Russia. Ami's hyperkinesis was made clear, and treatment for other dogs was made possible by Samuel Corson's landmark work at Ohio State University's biopsychiatry department. Meanwhile, we wrote case records, many of which were published in *Modern Veterinary Practice* magazine. I was privileged to lecture at UCLA in extension programs conducted by the late Herbert Snow, DVM.

When the first edition of *Behavior Problems in Dogs* appeared in 1975, an avalanche of new interest in pet dog behavior sprung up among veterinarians, dog trainers, breeders, behaviorists, and even some psychiatrists and psychologists. I wanted to think the reason for all this interest was the correction methods I recommended: No physical punishment, scolding or prolonged close confinement. They were humane and scientifically sound. However, with few exceptions, I was wrong. The idea that really caught on concerned a new field of endeavor . . . one that offered people interested in dog behavior a very good living. New books could be written; new departments established at veterinary colleges; new career opportunities opened for veterinarians, trainers, behavioral biologists, and psychologists. All this and more has come to pass.

Naturally, that diverse, new wave of experts entering the field brought along their experience and training. The ironic result was that new modes of punishment, force, and coldly "scientific" conditioning techniques have since been increasingly inflicted on hapless problem dogs. Today, dog owners are offered a vast array of abusive behavioral corrections, training techniques and hi-tech gadgetry. You can choose from hitting or wrestling your dog into submission, hanging him by the choke collar until he goes limp, even shocking his throat with up to several hundred volts. Or you can listen to that inner voice that says, "This animal is a family companion. We don't hurt our companions. There must be a better, kinder way."

I'll tell you no lies in these pages. I won't tell you that dogs are "denning" animals, so crate training your dog is "natural." That's not the truth. The only denning dog or wolf is a pregnant bitch. And when she and her pups leave their dens, they are plainly joyful to be out of it! I won't tell you to shake your puppy by the scruff of the neck as punishment because "that's what dog mothers do." That is not the truth. Bitches don't shake their puppies. Shaking puppies or babies can seriously injure them. I won't call electric shock "stimulation." That's not the whole truth. Instead, I will advise you to put a shock collar on your own neck. You'll quickly learn the difference between stimulation and pain. I won't tell you that a shock collar can keep your dog "safe" in an unfenced yard. That's not the truth. Not only have dogs "busted out" of their electronic fences, they have severely mauled and nearly killed neighborhood children. I won't tell you that dogs are dummies. That's a downright lie. I've seen dogs solve practical problems that would defy solutions by eight-year-old kids. I've seen dogs sense danger when their owners didn't recognize it when it was staring them in the face. I've met a dog who rescued his owner from drowning in heavy surf that kept grown men on the beach.

Dogs are amazing animals. They possess incredible learning abilities that don't require tidbits or pain for motivation. All they need is a teacher who understands them, someone who knows that humans don't yet know all there is to know about the depth of the dogs' potential.

Family pets don't choose us. We choose them. When they misbehave, the first thing they need is our understanding about why they do so. Then they need corrections that apply new insights about the nobler instinctive and learned behavior of both the human and canine species. More simply stated, our dogs are at our mercy, and that's what they need. That's what this book is about: truth and mercy.

William E. Campbell
Grants Pass, Oregon

P.S. After following our advice, if you don't reach your goals, read and heed the chapter *Selecting a Behavior Consultant*. It will save time, effort, money, and the unexpected grief of exposing your dog to abusive treatment.

UNDERSTANDING YOUR DOG

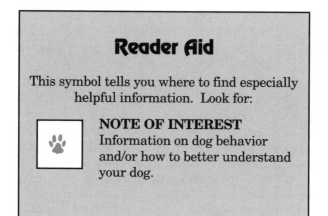

Reader Aid

This symbol tells you where to find especially helpful information. Look for:

NOTE OF INTEREST
Information on dog behavior and/or how to better understand your dog.

Understanding Dog Behavior

When you are trying to housetrain a new puppy, correct an adult dog from soiling in the house or solve a destructive chewing problem, you will be successful far more quickly if you understand how your dog thinks. If you know this, you can appreciate how the dog learns. Armed with this knowledge you can use methods that communicate humanely, naturally and effectively. So let's investigate the mind of the dog.

How Dogs Think

First we have to ask if dogs think at all. Some experts are of the opinion that dogs don't think, they merely behave. However, the popular definitions of thinking, *"to form or have in mind"* and *"to intend, plan"* certainly fit the way dogs behave. They *plan* to get petted when they approach us and nudge for it. They *have in mind* greeting us when they wag their tails and go to the door when they hear our car pull into the garage, etc. They may not think in the complex, abstract way as do we humans, but they certainly think nonverbally. A famous learning scientist who worked with flatworm behavior said, "If you're going to study flatworm behavior, you'd better learn to think like a flatworm." With this attitude, he made notable contributions to the mechanics of learning in all animals. With this principle in mind, we'll consider evidence about how dogs think. When we gain some insight about this, the various ways to influence their behavior become infinitely more understandable and appealing than simply trying to influence their behavior.

One thing seems certain: Dogs don't think in verbal language. They have never been seen sitting around in groups, making well-defined noises, as if having a chat. The noises they make usually relate to emotional expressions or attempts to gain attention, as in barking angrily at another dog approaching their property, or woofing at the back door to get us to let them into the house. So, if they don't use words to think, what do they use?

Images and Senses

The most appealing evidence suggests that dogs think in images and other sensory impressions, such as sounds and odors. This is not to say that they sit around on quiet days experiencing videos inside their brains. However, they likely share our ability to form in their minds images and experience certain odors and sounds. A scientific basis for this idea came from Russia and was published in the United States in 1973. A scientist named Rusinov was studying the electrophysiology of the brain and had several dogs permanently wired with brain-wave equipment and radio transmitters. When the dogs were brought into the lab from the kennels for experimental conditioning tests, the electroencephalograph machine was turned on and recorded their brain-wave patterns. This was done at the same time each day, five days a week. Purely by accident, one weekend Rusinov brought a group of visitors into the lab and turned on the EEG machine. Lo, the dog that was on schedule for tests at that time was sending wave forms nearly identical to his weekday working patterns! When the testing time passed, the dog's brain waves soon returned to normal, "at rest" forms. I never found any mention by Rusinov as to whether the dogs out in the kennel were actually performing their laboratory-conditioned behaviors. Chances are they were not, but one thing is almost sure: They were apparently experiencing them mentally. However, Rusinov's work showed that his dogs could keep a biological clock on such experiences. It was found to be accurate to within thirty seconds in a twenty-four-hour time period!

The late Polish scientist, Jerzi Konorski, taught dogs to salivate and expect food in their trays when a light flickered. This was done regularly every few mintues. However, after a few trials, the dogs started salivating and looking at the trays as if the food were actually there even though the light had not flickered. Konorski ventured that the dogs were hallucinating about both the stimulus (the light) and the reward for salivating (the food). One thing is certain: Something was happening in the dogs' minds that made them *behave* as if the actual experiences were occurring.

Some Human Examples

Before going on with dogs, let's think about our own "mind's eye." Imagine we have a date to meet someone we are particularly fond of at a busy restaurant. We arrive a few minutes early and sit a table near the door. The appointed time goes by and we begin to wonder if they are coming. We start watching people approach the door. Pretty soon, even those with similar features almost cause us to call out to them. Most of us have had these experiences, just as thinking about a loved one often conjures up a brief mental image of them. This often applies to the sound of their voice as well. Think about your favorite musical piece and your can almost "hear" it. These are all positive images. They are emotionally pleasant. On the other hand, recalling terrifying experiences can not only create their images, but even make us shudder. This is an example of negative images. They are emotionally unpleasant.

It is important to remember that we humans can discuss the nature of our mental impressions about life and the people around us. When Peggy, my wife, leaves for town on a stormy day and says, "I'll be back in a few minutes," then gets bogged down with some errand for several hours without calling to let me know, I get concerned. I might even imagine she has been in an accident. I start going to the window when cars slow down in front of the house. In a word, I am anxious. When she finally does get home, I'm happy and relieved. So it is with our dogs. When we are late getting home, or if they over-miss us because we have spoiled them, they worry in images. They probably can't abstractly imagine (form images of) car accidents, but they *can* recall images of us and our activities at home, such as fluffing the pillows on the sofa, putting away record albums, handling magazines and books, putting on shoes just before leaving, sitting in a favorite armchair, etc. As a result, when we are gone, they often engage in activities which involve them with these articles or activities. So the pillows may wind up on the floor, albums or magazines may be moved or chewed, a chair seat dug up, shoes brought out of the closet. The dogs want our presence and try to experience things which are symbolic of us.

While our dogs cannot think verbally about life's experiences, it is likely these experiences are stored as images in their memory banks and are responsible for much of the dogs' behavior, or misbehavior.

Now consider the new puppy whose owner comes home regularly and joins in the ecstatic joy of the typical greeting ceremony. As this becomes ingrained, the dog begins anticipating the experience.

As will happen in even the most well-regulated household, one day the owner is late. The puppy begins fretting, pacing. Well-primed energies begin demanding an outlet. What's going on in his mind? Probably, in his mind's eye or ear, he imagines hearing footsteps, perhaps even seeing the door open . . . which doesn't happen. But it should. This introduces a conflict between what the puppy expects and reality. Conflict creates frustration. Frustration produces anxiety, which produces a rush of adrenalin, which produces activity. The pup searches for something to satisfy his desire to "experience" the owner. He comes upon a magazine or book he saw the owner reading recently. It is rich with the owner's scent. If he cannot have the owner's presence, he can at least have the odor, even the taste. So he sniffs, tastes, sometimes even swallows parts of the article. Of course, none of this fully substitutes for the whole owner, so we can't say the puppy's desires are fully satified.

Then comes the owner. The puppy innocently launches into the joyous, semi-hysterical ritual. The owner starts to join in, but spies the magazine or book, now torn to shreds. Quite naturally, if not wisely, the owner angrily grabs the pup, drags him to the pulverized object and scolds or slaps his snout or rump, or both. The pet's single-track attention is riveted on the owner. He yips, rolls over or

The dog gets uptight and tense when the house is like a morgue.

Isolation fear.

tries vainly to escape. The owner, growling, picks up the remnants of the article and storms to the trash basket. The confused pup now has a brand new, conflicting image of his owner. This sort of shock to the nervous system, both in animals and humans, is called *psychic trauma*. A conflict has been instilled between the positive image of the owner (happy Dr. Jekyll) and the negative (Mr. Homecoming Hyde). The conflict creates frustration and anxiety about homecomings, especially when this treatment is repeated a few times. Since the punishment was not associated with the act of chewing up something, the puppy seeks out another article, perhaps a shoe, and the punishment cycle is repeated until the relationship between owner and dog is now emotionally ambivalent. They have mixed feelings about each other. Their relationship is deteriorating. The owner often concludes the punishment was not severe enough. That's why the correction was not permanent. So he intensifies it. The relationship erodes further as weeks go by. Enough of this cascading, negative effect and the owner is ready take drastic action. The maturing pup, now highly sensitized to his owner's mood change, feels something is wrong. This can often be reflected by new problems, such as submissive wetting when the owner comes home or approaches at other times, off-schedule bowel movements or urination, etc. The puppy acts insecure, currying more favor when the owner is home, but missing the owner even more acutely when left alone. Frustration and anxiety build while the isolation-related, tension-relieving behavior mounts.

The unwitting owner, who originally may have thought the pup was "getting even" for being left alone, begins to consider the now maturing dog as incorrigible. Outside help is sought. A book may be purchased. A veterinarian, breeder, pet shop, or trainer may be consulted. The dog may wind up in a cramped crate or cage all day, in the yard or garage, or with his mouth stuffed with chewed debris and taped shut for hours. Or, too often, he may end up at the local pound with a potential life span of another five to seven days.

Is this because the owner was not aware of how dogs think? Probably not. It is more likely due to ignorance of the dog's needs. However, with an understanding of how our dogs think, let's analyze the key behavioral elements of housetraining a puppy or older dog to see how it is applied. We'll take it in a series of steps.

Housetraining: A Positive Framework

1. **Teach the dog that you are his leader and teacher.** Each time the pup seeks your affection, have him sit for a few seconds. Praise and pet, then release him. This instills positive feelings about following your instructions.
2. **Positively reinforce proper behavior.** After eating, drinking water, excitement, chewing for more than a few minutes or awakening, even from a nap, shoo him to his toilet place and stand still. When he does his duty, go to the spot and point at the "stuff," saying, "Good toilet" or some other name you choose. Present positive impressions of the "stuff" at the proper place. If you catch the dog starting to sniff or posturing to "go" in the house, clap your hands once, or knock once on a table top or wall, and immediately praise with "Good dog" the interruption in his thinking about urinating or defecating.

3. Avoid the negative. When you find an accident, ignore it. Shoo the pup to the proper toilet place. If he performs there, praise, point and pet as before. If he doesn't perform, leave him there if possible and clean up the mess without the pup present. If you can't leave him, put him where he cannot see you clean up. This avoids negative interaction between you and the puppy regarding his natural functions.

These are just a few elements in a housetraining program that succeeds as quickly as two to four days in ideal situations. You probably noticed that these steps form positive mental images for the dog and avoid negative ones. This simple principle underlies all the correction and teaching methods to follow. But before getting specific about these, we must examine more of the inner mental workings of dogs.

"Up, Boy! Up on the table! He does it all the time at home.
Up! Up!

Natural Reactions of the Dog

Reflexes

Reflexes are gifts from nature (inborn or unconditioned) or the result of experience (learned or conditioned). Without reflexes we couldn't get up in the morning or swallow food. A textbook would be needed to describe all the dog's reflexes, so I will mention only those that bear on the development of problems or their corrections.

11

Pavlov and Conditioned
versus Unconditioned Reflexes

Years ago, a Russian investigator of reflexes, Ivan Pavlov, put dogs on tables, harnessed them securely and taught them various things, among which was to salivate when he rang a bell. The dogs quickly learned this trick because they were usually hungry when the experiments started, and were given food shortly after the bell rang. Salivating for food is called an unconditioned (not learned) reflex, while drooling for the bell is a conditioned (learned) reflex. Pavlov's studies helped to classify reflexes in a way that is useful in understanding dog problems. One thing Pavlov noticed was that all the dogs struggled, some mildly, some wildly, when they were first put into harness. So impressed was he about this reflex that he called it the "freedom reflex." The important thing about this reflex is that its strength tends to relate directly to how excitable the dog is. Excitability is a condition Pavlov attributed to the whole nervous system, especially the brain. He measured it by testing how strongly dogs reacted to various stimuli. At the other end of the scale was how quickly dogs' nervous systems quit reacting to stimuli, which Pavlov called inhibition.

Pavlov's Principles

Though we may disagree with many of Pavlov's methods, one of which was to create grossly neurotic dogs, his studies did produce useful information. Here are some of Pavlov's helpful findings:

- Excitable dogs are easier to upset emotionally and make neurotic.

- Excitable dogs go crazy actively—outwardly, a condition called "manic."

- Dogs with "balanced" nervous systems are more difficult to unbalance emotionally.

- Inhibited dogs are more difficult to make neurotic.

- Inhibited dogs react inwardly when they are emotionally unbalanced, becoming "depressed."

These principles should be kept in mind when you are selecting a pup or testing your own puppy with the handling test described in the Puppy Primer section. Which type gets along best in what type of environment is an important consideration in avoiding behavior problems. Pavlov and his followers also documented many important things about how dogs learn. Here are two of those:

HOW DOGS LEARN

- Learned (conditioned) behavior requires six weeks of regular teaching before it tends to be permanent.

- Most dogs need to be taught in several different locations, with increasing distractions, before they can perform a task dependably. This explains why your dog might sit nicely for you at home or in the yard, but seems to "go deaf" when you get to the veterinarian's office. Don't blame the dog. Teach him to sit in different locations over a six-week period and you can solve the problem.

Defense Reflexes

Defense reflexes become evident when the dog perceives a threat to his well-being. It is important to understand that all of us and our pets possess an ultimate expression of defensive behavior that will surface when faced with physical harm. This natural endowment is not a character flaw in man or animal. It is merely a fact of life. Faced with a threat, a dog will either fight, flee, or freeze. If you decide physical punishment is the way to correct undesirable behavior, and your dog is a passive, freeze-type, it will probably require only the mildest sign of a physical threat to get your point across. A flight-type will retreat, but might well bite, if held or cornered for punishment, since he can't escape. The fight-type may tolerate a certain amount of harsh treatment, but beware! Nature will out. Sooner or later you may need to settle the issue with a club, or you may find yourself in the emergency ward for some expensive stitchery. There is also another tragic possibility. Many fight-type dogs suppress their active-aggressive defense tendencies with the person who punishes them, but will not do so if someone else (often a family child) makes what the dog perceives

"Give her one tranquilizing tablet before guests arrive, two before riding in the car, and eight before she comes to me again."

as a menacing move. This can result in an injured child and a dead pet dog, victimized by a sad combination of its basic nature and human ignorance.

Fortunately there are alternatives to force and punishment. I have helped hundreds of owners achieve satisfying lives with active (fight or flight) defense reflex dogs with never a sign of such misplaced aggression. We simply work with the causes for problems rather than punish the symptoms.

Defensive Biting

A bite can be suffered when someone blows air into a dog's ear. A dog will even bite a bicycle pump if it is used for this purpose. Sadly, many little human faces are scarred every year because children hug dogs around the neck and innocently exhale a gleeful puff into the pet's ear. Most dogs learn to inhibit this bite reflex, but, even so, the best policy is child-training against breathing into even the most docile dog's ear.

Anything that moves quickly into a dog's field of vision can also stimulate a defensive bite reflex. This accounts for most of the oral bee stings dogs suffer. Just as a human baby grabs with its hand things that suddenly appear, so we adults will instinctively, by reflex, catch a ball unexpectedly tossed to us. Unfortunately, the dog's equipment for catching things is full of teeth! As a result, many well-meaning people get nipped while reaching to exchange a little affection with the new puppy, which can lead to severe punishment for the pup, unless the owner is enlightened.

Having looked at the simple defensive bite reflexes, let's now consider the overall canine nervous system and see how it's wired for reflexes, both inborn and learned, and how a dog's general excitability (nervousness) affects behavior problems and their corrections.

The Orienting Reflex

It is of little use merely to say that the orienting reflex serves to alert your dog to changes in the environment unless I describe the kinds of things that trigger the reflex, what effect they have on the dog's mental processes and how they can take part in causing or correcting behavior problems.

Man, dogs and all other normal mammals share this life-saving orienting reflex. It operates through all our senses to let us know something outside, on, or even inside our bodies has changed. A simpler name for it is the "What's that?" reflex. The internal effect of this reflex is an extremely brief interruption of ongoing mental activity plus, in the case of an outside-the-body change, attention (orienting) toward the source of the change, or stimulus. Without the orienting reflex we wouldn't notice dangerous things like approaching cars until we felt the crunch of a collision.

Immediately following the orienting reflex comes the mental process of locating and interpreting the nature of the stimulus so that a decision can be made as to whether or not to do something about it, such as putting on the brakes and avoiding an approaching car. The sensitivity of the orienting reflex depends on our degree of alertness. It is nearly dormant when we slumber, so a very strong stimulus is required to trigger it. On the other hand, when we are "wound up" about things, even a very weak stimulus (someone lightly touching our shoulder) can startle us, and a strong stimulus can cause our hearts to skip a beat or two.

With super-keen senses, dogs are especially reactive to their orienting reflexes. This provides us with a marvelous tool for teaching simple things like come, sit, and stay without leashes or

The orienting reflex alerts the dog to life's hazards.

the need to touch the dogs. More important, though, is that the orienting reflex opens a virtual pathway to our dogs' emotions, because the orienting reflex is followed by other reflexes for locating, interpreting and deciding what, if anything, to do, or how to feel about the stimulus that started the whole chain of reactions. If we learn how to affect and change the way a dog feels about things, we'll have the secret to solving even severe problems. Let's take a case and see how it works.

Aggressive Behavior

You have a dog that shows extreme aggression toward visitors. One visitor has been bitten. We won't bother now to consider how this problem developed, only what you have done to try to control it. You started by answering the door and holding the dog's collar, petting and speaking soothingly to reassure the dog. That didn't work. In fact it made things worse. So you tried negative-feedback routines: You scolded, spanked, put the dog on a leash. The dog's ferocity grew wilder. Now you put the dog out or in a separate room when folks come to call.

AGGRESSION TOWARDS VISITORS

CAUSE

EFFECT

All these steps failed for the following reasons: Petting and reassuring tones were interpreted by the dog as approval of his feelings of hostility and aggressive behavior, so things got worse due to positive reinforcement. Then the heavy-handed stuff failed because the dog associated the arrival of people with your disapproval. The ultimate negative was to be excluded from the "pack." These treatments were negative. Now the situation is so bad that your dog starts barking and charging the door when he hears footsteps out front, or when a car door slams, both of which signal possible visitor arrivals. To make matters even more complicated, the dog has started growling at you when you grab his collar to take him to the other room or outdoors. Now you're afraid you may get bitten!

The Interpretive Factor

So, now what to do? Since your pet's nasty behavior is a result of his feelings of hostility, the solution lies in changing his emotional interpretation of the situation. This must start well before he is facing people at the door. Fortunately, you have one vitally important emotional element in your favor. Your dog loves to play ball about as much as he hates the arrival of visitors. This will be important when using the orienting reflex and interpretive factor. Here is the sequence of events in a correctional setup.

The chain of reconditioning the dog's emotional and behavioral reaction goes like this:

- You have an accomplice outside start approaching the door.

- Footsteps occur; dog alerts; footsteps instantly stop.

- Instantly after dog alerts, you clap hands, bounce ball, happily move about and invite dog to play, until he takes part.

(The hand-clap and ball-bounce cause an orienting reflex, which interrupts the dog's impending hostility. The happy movement and upbeat invitation provide a new interpretive factor—one of jolliness.)

The Jolly Routine

The foregoing procedure is called the "Jolly Routine." It is used to correct most of the serious, emotionally based problems, including fearfulness. The Jolly Routine must be applied while gradually bringing the footsteps closer to the house, until the guests can arrive at the door and take part in the ball game.

The Jolly Routine.

Warning: There is much more to correcting aggressive behavior than merely applying this Jolly Routine. First you need to gain a position of emotional leadership with your dog. Otherwise you could be running around bouncing the ball while the dog is trying to tear the front door off the hinges!

The Chase Reflex

The chase reflex appears almost as soon as pups are able to move around on all fours. Anything that moves fast is doomed to get pursued and pounced upon. This is invaluable for developing prey-catching skills in the wild, but it gets downright exasperating when practiced on human ankles and clothing around the house. It becomes genuinely vexing when it graduates to the outdoors and is

triggered by bicycles, cars and running people. This predatory, game-chasing reflex does not have an emotional base in most cases, but it requires extra portions of patience, effort and time for correction, as will be seen in the Chasing correction program.

The Resistance Reflex

Numerous reflexes combine to keep a dog's body in any particular position—standing, sitting, lying down, or in any stage of movement. One that is useful with problem dogs and for teaching certain types of behavior is called *positive thigmotaxis*. For clarity, we'll call it the "resistance" reflex. You can test it in your dog by gently pressing against the side of the rump while he is standing. That pressure pushing back at you is caused by positive thigmotaxis. If, instead of pushing back, the dog gives way, you have stimulated negative thigmotaxis, a rare response except in dogs having severely inhibited nervous systems or those suffering from kennelosis due to isolation from normal social contacts during puppyhood. Understanding the push-back reflex helps avoid and solve some problems. For instance, the best way to stop a pesky dog from leaning against you is not to push him away, which can stimulate a stronger lean by the dog. Rather, suddenly remove the part of your anatomy being leaned on. This will upset the dog's balance and he will either collapse onto the floor with indignity, or the righting reflex will jolt him upright again. Enough of this, with praise when he quits leaning, and you've solved the problem. Be sure to do this in several locations and every time the leaning occurs. One "unbalancing" lesson doesn't necessarily solve the problem.

This reflex is also the main reason that dogs make great sled, wagon and bicycle pullers. Unfortunately, the same holds true as people-pullers. The sight of owners being hauled down the street by their pets is incredibly common and often downright comical. It is surprising how quickly most leash-strainers can be permanently corrected in the early stages of their careers if you start with a loose leash and turn and walk in the opposite direction every time the dog starts to get ahead of you, saying his name as you do so. If we consider this reflex with the freedom reflex, it's easy to understand how tethers and tight leashes can cause frustration and aggression in dogs. In fact, for some dogs, fences alone create enough frustration to result in severe aggression toward people or other animals beyond reach.

If a puppy makes a mistake just growl at it!

Eating and Elimination Reflexes

Puppies are born with reflexes that cause them to root toward warmth and to suckle on just about anything resembling a nipple. This and a swallow reflex make the newborns well equipped to get nourishment into their bodies, but nature neglected to give them a reflex to eliminate wastes. A human baby's full bladder sends a message to its urinary sphincter, and that muscle relaxes to relieve the pressure. Not so with newborn pups. They require that their mother lick them around the genitals and anus to stimulate elimination, otherwise they would die of blood poisoning due to blockage of urine flow from the kidneys. The same maternal licking also causes the rectum to evacuate solid wastes. This quirk of nature, used properly, makes housetraining a puppy a simple matter compared to potty-training a child. The reflex to urinate or defecate can be absolutely predictable in pups and adult dogs. These reflexes are vital to our quick, effective housetraining programs.

Thus, we see that a dog's reflexes are natural reactions to what he senses from both outside and inside his body. There are some significant differences between man and dog, and understanding them will help immensely in understanding and correcting canine behavior.

How Dogs
Sense Their World

Anyone who wants to understand canine behavior had better learn to think like a dog. This seems far-fetched, but it is true. If we don't understand that the dog sees, hears, smells, tastes, and touches a world that is perceived somewhat differently from ours, it will be impossible to develop insight about canine

23

behavior. Without this knowledge, any attempts to train, shape new behavior, or change existing behavior, must be limited to outmoded carrot-and-stick techniques. It doesn't require a lot of study, but with the dog's mind in mind, a whole range of problems can be avoided and solved quickly and humanely.

Vision

Canine eyesight is poor compared to ours when it comes to color perception or identifying shapes or details within a form (such as noses on faces), yet dogs can see things when we would say it is totally dark. They can perceive movements so subtle that we'd swear there was none. Their wide-angle vision is about twice ours, while their focus-vision is narrower. If you remember that nature equipped our pets to survive as predators, these variations make sense. A slight movement of a single blade of grass at gathering dusk is detected by the peripheral vision, causing eyes and head to turn almost to the exact spot where the field mouse moved. So begins the stalk for dinner.

This sensitivity to subtle movement helps explain how our pets often seem to know when we are about to get up to leave the house, get dinner ready, or go to bed. We unconsciously make

Canine eyesight is poor when compared to humans.

minute movements before taking deliberate actions. Dogs are astute people-watchers, using their extra-keen visual talents to keep up with or, at times, ahead of us.

On the minus side, poor shape, form and detail vision may cause some dogs to become uneasy and even to freak out when they see their owners for the first time wearing a hat, using crutches, carrying a pole, or approaching in semi-darkness. This is why it's a wise policy to speak in an upbeat tone of voice to your dog (or a strange one, too) in these circumstances.

If you have a dog with hair that hangs over its eyes, do your pet a favor and tie it up or, better yet, cut it off. Life down on the floor is tough enough without having to look at the world through a picket fence. This avoids visual surprises when people reach to pet or pick up the dog. Contrary to popular myth, "hairy-eyed" dogs do not go blind when their eyes are exposed to sunlight. These are the important visual perception differences between us.

Smell

You and I can't even imagine possessing an odor-sensor that can detect a human body buried under a snow avalanche for days or identify a chemical diluted in a million parts of water. This exquisite sense makes an evening walk a veritable mental feast for our pets, not just physical exercise. Noses create problems, too, because dogs have a strong drive to investigate odors, especially if the smell is airborne. Many runaway problems start with these.

Our pets use this olfactory sense to identify us and other people and animals. We all exude airborne chemicals from every pore and opening in our bodies. The ones that beget specific responses from kindred animals are called pheromones. For example, a female dog about to come into heat emits messages that can attract male dogs from miles around. Around people, most pet dogs are content to sniff at a respectable distance for identity odors. However, if they move in close to someone's crotch for more detail, or jump up to gain access to life's very essence, our breath, they violate human values and find themselves in big trouble. Most such offenders, if caught early enough in their careers, can be corrected—if enough people crouch down to greet them. After a few meetings with several people the dogs are usually content to settle for less intimate introductions.

He probably smells your dog on you.

Hearing

Another dog sense that dwarfs its human counterpart is hearing. Footsteps that a keen-eared person can't detect from sixty feet away are heard by dogs when the walker is at least four times that distance. We really shouldn't be too surprised when our pet starts getting excited before the family car rolls into the driveway or if the barking begins long before the doorbell rings. Most dogs also seem able to hear selectively from among all sorts of sounds and detect those that are important to them. You'll see this when your dog alerts toward something outdoors when the TV is blaring away in the same room. Ultrasonic frequencies, at least twice as high as those we can hear, are picked up easily by dogs. This is why silent dog whistles and other ultrasonic devices cause an orienting reflex in dogs. Most dogs do not find such sounds unpleasant unless they are extremely loud.

With this exquisite sense, if you want to train a reliable watchdog, don't shush him when he barks at what you cannot hear. Instead, help him investigate by cautiously going toward the source of the sound. If it is some normal neighborhood sound, such as kids on skateboards, act nonchalant and show the dog there is nothing to get excited about. But, when unusual sounds occur (for example, have a friend softly jimmy a door or window), lead the dog to the scene and get excited yourself. This will help him learn the difference between OK and not-OK noises, thus avoiding the racket of a dog that barks at everything.

Even with this hearing sensitivity, dogs are not particularly talented at discriminating different qualities or characteristics of sounds, especially those of human language. This can lead to many problems between people and their pets. Thus there are folks with disobedient dogs who say, "He understands every word I say, but he's just being stubborn!" This is not necessarily so. While dogs' hearing nerves connect with brain centers functionally akin to human sound centers, unlike persons, they do not develop anything like our language and speech centers. This is possibly because their voice boxes do not function like ours, and their tongues, lips and mouths are not shaped properly for the kind of speech we develop.

One way to appreciate the dog's perception of our spoken language is to join a foreign language class that uses the conversational

Hi-fi hearing!

approach, rather than the reading method, and forbids students to use English in the classroom. A lot of pointing, touching, moving about, posturing and facial expressions will be used before you learn to do the right things when the teacher looks at you and says, "Venay! Ah-say-yay-voo! Res-tay!" When you finally do get it, you know that when the teacher makes those sounds you're supposed to come, sit, and stay, in that order. You also appreciate how important the teacher's expressions of approval are, especially when you start to take the first step toward her in response to the sound "venay." The expressions of approval (praise) let you know you are thinking about the right thing and motivate you to continue toward the teacher with enthusiasm. With such positive, socially rewarding systems, people learn basic commands in French almost as quickly as they are learned by dogs! The dog's advantage is his extreme sensitivity to posture and movement cues and his positive responses to approval in the form of praise and petting.

Taste

Dogs are not burdened with social values regarding what is or is not proper to put in their mouths, so just about anything that isn't burning gets tasted and often swallowed. This includes rotten meat, garbage, bugs, and that ultimate no-no—stools (not the kind

Discriminating taste.

you sit on!). Though furniture, shoes, clothing, carpets, and the like are also on some dogs' lists of edibles, these nonfood items satisfy a psychological, rather than physical, appetite. Suffice it to say a dog's sense of taste is probably as good as his sense of smell, and both can get a pet into trouble around the house.

Touch

Touch (tactile) senses play a vital role in understanding behavior problems. Not only does *where* you touch a dog have basic meaning, but *how* you touch is important, too. Canine and human nervous systems are designed with one basic aim, the propagation of the species. To propagate, we must survive; to survive we need to get water, food, and shelter, avoid crippling injury or getting devoured by another meat-eater, and respond appropriately to sexual stimulation.

Prolonged petting can send a mixed message.

Let's consider this vital tactile sense and some basic reflexes necessary to survival and propagation as they lead to canine behavior problems. An unexpected touch on the muzzle, head, neck, or body (especially from the withers to the base of the skull) triggers a brain-stem reflex to bite. From an evolutionary view this is important. In the wild, even an instant's hesitation between touch and defensive action, such as turning to see if friend or foe has pounced, might result in serious injury or an unpleasant trip as a lion's dinner.

Fortunately for us and our pets, nervous systems don't stop at the top of the spine with the brain stem. We both have more elaborate, higher brain centers that can control (inhibit) such basic reflexes. Without these, dogs or babies could never be housetrained. Through gentle handling by persons, dogs learn to control the primitive defensive bite reflex and usually respond affectionately when touched, except when they are drowsy or asleep. Hence the saying, "Let sleeping dogs lie," which unfortunately not all parents teach their children. Such lack of training leads to thousands of dog bites every year and a trip to the pound for many innocent animals.

Another defensive reflex is activated when the paws or legs of the dog are touched, especially unexpectedly. The response is to withdraw the limb. This seems logical for survival, since withdrawal insures the dog's ability to take whatever action may be required, such as walking gingerly through a thorn patch.

These and other defensive reflexes to be mentioned later occur in varying degrees in different dogs, even from the same litter of pups. Proper handling helps a pet learn to control them, but improper handling can actually strengthen them and confuse the dog. For instance, the touch-bite reflex makes clear how counterproductive it can be to swat a "mouthy" puppy across the snout. A more sensible correction would be to trigger the withdrawal reflex by grabbing a paw and praising the pup when he starts to get mouthy. This approach avoids the negative aspects that punishment can introduce to the relationship between owner and dog.

Courtship Behavior

People don't have a monopoly on foreplay. In dogs it is called *courtship behavior*, with lots of tail wagging, play invitations, and running together. There is also a great deal of touching, especially nosing around the ears and neck, leaning on one another, and, sometimes, putting the forepaws on the other's back. It is interesting that almost every form of courtship behavior occurs within litters of puppies, as dominant behavior, well before puberty. Some pups respond to a human wrist or leg touching their throats or chests by firmly clasping their forelegs thereto and performing vigorous pelvic thrusts. Most people don't abide this behavior, so they withdraw the arm or leg and/or either scold or punish the puppy. Fortunately, most dogs control their sex drives early among a human family. However, prolonged petting can send a mixed message and release some arousing hormones and the dogs (male or female) can experience considerable frustration trying to keep themselves under control.

Pain

The sense of pain is closely associated with touch. Puppies raised in normal litters and transplanted to human families usually develop normal pain responses. But if a pup is raised in isolation from other living things, his pain perception can be severely hampered, along with other capabilities. For instance, when first exposed to an open flame, isolation-raised puppies may continually stick their noses into it, even until blisters appear. They also fail to avoid objects moving toward them, even though these cause pain to normally raised pups.

Prolonged isolation, beyond three or four months of age, causes many pups develop a condition called *kennelosis*. Like zombies, these pups barely react to anything. It is important to remember that dogs depend heavily on other living things for normal perceptive and emotional development. That's why lots of socialization is vital for puppies.

Direction

A dog's sense of direction may not be as sharp as a homing pigeon's, but it certainly beats man's all hollow. Well-confirmed stories abound of dogs leading their hopelessly befuddled owners safely home through blinding snowstorms. Which sensory system makes these uncanny abilities possible is not known, but they can also be troublesome during the housetraining of a puppy or older dog. Dogs have to learn the route to their toilet area before they are dependably housetrained. If they have to move north from the food bowl, turn west around the corner, then south to the back door, where it's west out the door and then north to the toilet area, they are faced with a literal maze-learning problem. Since the first and final legs of the journey are northward, many unsupervised dogs take a directional shortcut and wind up relieving themselves close to the north wall, but inside the house. This is as close as they can get to the toilet area using a canine compass.

Balance

The sense of balance keeps both people and dogs on their respective feet. Dogs can learn to walk tightropes and walk on either front or rear legs, alien as these feats are to the way they are built. Balance is important in only one serious problem, that of car-sickness. Even then the cause is more often emotional than physical. There is one problem that balance can help in preventing or correcting, that of getting up on furniture. If a dog never is to be allowed on furniture, just move the furniture back and forward when he jumps up so as to upset the dog's balance. If you can do it so the dog doesn't realize you're the cause, so much the better. A few "unbalancing" sessions usually create a dependable, floor-model dog.

Extrasensory Perceptions

All animals have biological clocks, but pet dogs seem to develop an uncanny sense about when things like getting up, going for regular walks, feeding times, and their owners' leaving and homecoming times are due to happen. In dogs, this sense has been scientifically demonstrated to be accurate to within about thirty seconds in a twenty-four-hour period. This can be one of the causes for problems associated with being left alone by a guilt-ridden owner, often called "separation anxiety," or homecomings, when there is a lot of emotion.

Extrasensory abilities are baffling enough when they occur in people. In our nonverbal dogs, they are even more confounding. Problems may or may not be definitely related to ESP, but here is some food for thought concerning the dog's ability to anticipate storms and earthquakes, as well as to detect people's emotional states.

Some dogs get restless and exhibit whining or pacing hours or even days before thunderstorms or earthquakes occur. It is theorized that they somehow sense changes in humidity, barometric pressure, or the positive-to-negative ratio of the air's ionization. Some dogs actually disappear well before clouds appear in the sky. My case files indicate that the more fearful and/or hysterical a dog gets when the storm hits, the better are his forecasting abilities. Correcting such dogs requires that their initial feelings of fear be dealt with; this may be hours before the storm hits and is when corrective steps must start. Effective correction of behavior problems deals primarily with a pet dog's emotional perception of situations. Once this emotional element is changed from negative to positive, the dog's behavior changes, often with no further effort on the owner's part.

Telepathy

Over the years I have seen demonstrations of a communications link between owners and their dogs that defy a scientific explanation. For instance, a young couple was at odds over the idea of getting rid of their ten-month-old female Shih Tzu. The husband was speaking angrily about the dog and her persistent house soiling. His wife was standing off to one side. The dog, sitting at her feet, could not see her mistress, whose cheeks were wet with tears. A moment later I noticed the Shih Tzu's eyes were watering.

In another case, a dog that was in our custody after his owner's death suddenly ripped up a favorite Micky Mouse squeaky toy given to him as a puppy by the owner. The dog had never chewed the toy during the several months he'd had it. In fact, he carried the toy around during the day and took it to bed with him at night. We later learned the time of the owner's burial two thousand miles away. It was the same as the time the dog destroyed the toy.

A somewhat scientific test for some sort of telepathy follows. A dog and his female owner lived in a close, healthy relationship for several years. The two were placed in separate rooms which were insulated from each other in every way scientifically known. A burly man entered the owner's room and started menacing her. (She had not been forewarned of this part of the experiment.) The lady was terrified. At that instant, in the isolated room where he had formerly rested quietly, the dog became extremely nervous and upset, whining, pacing, and seeking a way out.

These and other less scientific telepathic experiences abound in dog lore. Speculation as to how these occur ranges from "spiritual links," to undiscovered brain emanations that penetrate all known insulation methods and materials. This element may help to account for many problems I have seen which seem spontaneously to correct themselves after the owners, who had been thinking of getting rid of the pet, make a firm, emotional commitment to keep the dog no matter the consequences. Whatever the explanation, our dogs somehow sense our underlying emotional states. As we proceed, this rather mystical dimension is often the key to understanding and doing something about many behavior problems.

CANINE BEHAVIOR AND THE SENSES

Dogs are astute people-watchers. They anticipate our actions by noticing minute, subconscious movements we make.

Because their shape, form and detail vision is poor, dogs become unseasy when they see us in unusual costume or posture. Speak to the dog in an upbeat tone at these times.

The dog's extraordinary sense of smell invites him to investigate. Many runaways are drawn by an enticing airborne scent.

Dogs also have an acute sense of hearing and are able to hear selectively to detect those sounds that are important to them. Dogs pick up much higher frequencies than humans can hear.

Dogs have difficulty distinguishing between different characteristics of the human language. We can help by giving posture and movement cues and by praising.

Both a dog's sense of taste and smell entice him in ways that can get him into trouble when he responds to them according to instinct.

Unexpectedly touching the forepart of the body or the dog's head triggers biting. Unexpectedly touching the legs or feet causes withdrawal. Touching also stimulates the dog's sexual hormones.

Their keen sense of direction makes it easier to housetrain dogs if their toilet area is in a direct line from food bowl and door.

Dogs sense changes in weather and often get restless days before a major storm. Their biological clock tells them when it is time for their owners to leave or arrive home. Nervous or anxious behavior problems are often related to such events.

C H A P T E R 4

How Your Dog Communicates

Stance and movement speak volumes compared to the noises dogs make at each other or to people, though each is important in various situations. A low growl may be a warning to knock off some disturbing activity, or it can be a non-threatening pleasure sound when an otoscope is stuck in the ear for veterinary inspection.

When the growl comes from a dog standing with tail and hackles raised, however, the unmistakable message is that a battle could be in the offing. Besides the usual dominant and submissive postures and movements, dogs develop other ways to show submission and happiness by tail wagging, general excitability, prancing, and even jumping up and down. All of these fundamentals of dog talk are characterized in the following series of insightful cartoons.

Reactions to Threat

A pup or an older dog may react to perceived threats to his well-being by acting submissively in an effort to convey the idea, "OK, I give up. Please don't hurt me." If we recognize this, we should further realize that to press an already submitting dog with more severe threats or painful punishment is to change the rules of the canine dominance/submission ritual. This often creates enough perceived threat to cause the dog to react in his basic defensive nature. The result may be a pet that is a submissive wetter, a runaway, a fear-biter, or a dangerous, aggressive beast.

Eye Contact

People who stare at other people make them feel uncomfortable. This is true throughout the mammal world. Dogs are not exceptions. This sort of psychological, long-distance bullying can create problems in the basic relationships between owners and their dogs. Staring can also provoke a dog to bite when practiced with aggressive, strange dogs. Eye contact threats invite hostility where friendliness ought to exist.

RWW

FUNDAMENTAL DOG TALK

Dogs show submission and happiness by tail wagging, excitability, prancing, and jumping up and down.

FUNDAMENTAL DOG TALK

Play is invited or responded to by lowering the front end and raising the rump, tail up; or by prancing, running, and hopping about, waving a stiff foreleg at the "playee."

FUNDAMENTAL DOG TALK

A frontal approach with direct eye contact, tail and ears up, and hackles raised, is a sign that attack or a "bluff" is in the offing.

Circling another animal or person is dominant. Allowing it is somewhat submissive.

FUNDAMENTAL DOG TALK

A paw raised, with bent foreleg, is a submissive, friendly gesture.

FUNDAMENTAL DOG TALK

An absolutely still stance, with tail and ears up and the eyes rolled away, signals a readiness to fight, or that attack may be the next social gesture.

FUNDAMENTAL DOG TALK

A central position in a group can indicate a dog that either feels insecure, or feels he is the "leader" of the group.

FUNDAMENTAL DOG TALK

Insecure and/or overprotective dogs often "cut out" a stranger by walking or running between them and the family.

FUNDAMENTAL DOG TALK

A playful nip from the rear can mean a friendly "How-dee-do," or a mild form of objection to something that is going on.

FUNDAMENTAL DOG TALK

Taking a hand, arm, or leg and holding it in the mouth
signals a bossy dog.

Shoulder-bumping a person's
leg, especially when they first
start to walk somewhere, is the
sign of a bossy dog, although
some herding breeds do it with
no bossy intent.

FUNDAMENTAL DOG TALK

Direct eye contact, with or without expectant tail wagging, but with no aggressive signs, says, "Pay attention to me."

A nose "bunt" can signal a friendly greeting. It may also mean "thank you" after you give water to a thirsty dog.

FUNDAMENTAL DOG TALK

Nudging with the muzzle or nose says "Pet me."

Bossy dogs often take an outside position in a group, where they can "keep an eye" on everyone.

FUNDAMENTAL DOG TALK

"Come hither" movements tell us to follow.

FUNDAMENTAL DOG TALK

Some pets show their teeth in a kind of snarling smile, especially when greeting people. (I call this a "snile" or "smarl.") It is usually shown by submissive types and is often misunderstood as being aggressive.

A paw on the leg is generally a friendly invitation for petting or play, or means "Pay attention and await the next command!"

FUNDAMENTAL DOG TALK

Pet dogs adapt to and learn about human body language, too. If you crouch, especially sidewise toward a puppy or dog, they will usually approach in a friendly manner.

FUNDAMENTAL DOG TALK

When their owners stand or walk side by side with outsiders, most dogs interpret this as a friendly relationship.

FUNDAMENTAL DOG TALK

Face-to-face meetings between owners and outsiders may trigger aggression. This may be learned from witnessing family arguments, which are usually conducted from similar positions.

FUNDAMENTAL DOG TALK

When a stranger stands or sits within the family group, the dog may interpret it as pack invasion, even when people are side by side.

FUNDAMENTAL DOG TALK

Standing stock-still in the presence of an aggressive dog may trigger an attack. It is better to stand sideways to the dog, leaning slightly away from him, and turning smoothly with him if he starts to circle. Avoid locking into direct eye contact.

Social Development

All domestic puppies transfer their social tendencies from their own to the human pack. This is because of built-in reactions that appear shortly after birth. Let's look at some of them that lead to problems and also form the basis for many corrections of problems.

Life In The Litter

Urination and Defecation

Unlike human babies, puppies do not arrive with an independent physical mechanism for urinating or defecating. If their dam did not roll the pups onto their side or back and lick their genitals and anus to cause urination and defecation, they would soon die from the toxic effects of backed-up urine. After the roll-and-lick ritual, the good mother laps up the urine and eats the fecal material. This may seem disgusting, but healthy puppy waste is sterile, and this routine guarantees litter hygiene. It also creates a great mechanism for later housetraining, since the little ones develop a reflex habit of evacuating their waste matter shortly after eating or drinking.

Submissive Signals

Another reflex response to the mother's licking occurs as she cleans up about the youngsters' faces and throats; they raise their forepaws as if trying to fend off the attacking tongue. As she persists, most pups give up the battle and draw their forelegs into the sides of their chests in a kind of clasped knife position. Some even urinate. You can see both of these submissive responses in some adult dogs. A mild form occurs when a dog sits and raises a bent foreleg. In the litter situation, the pups have experienced their first exposure to dominance when the dam rolled them over for cleanup. At the same time the puppies have also, for the first time, displayed submission as a behavioral response.

Suckling and Swallowing Reflexes

Two other built-in reflexes are to suckle when hungry and to swallow when the suckled matter gets to a certain place in the mouth. Just like a human infant, a pup will try to get anything small enough into his mouth and give it a good working over. The reflex to root after anything warm and soft generally leads the pup to a nipple and nourishment. If he happens to get attached to a littermate's tail or foot, the mother will usually pull the errant puppy to the proper place. As the pups mature, their rooting and suckling reflexes fade, usually during the weaning stage. However, some adult dogs will suckle on blankets and even their owners' clothing when they feel emotionally insecure.

"Kissing" for Dinner

The weaning process begins about four weeks after birth. Many breeders force this process by taking the dam away from her litter. They usually provide a large tray of soft food so that the puppies are able to waddle to dinner. Other litters are naturally weaned, and the mother will often start to regurgitate some of her own food, which the young gobble up. After a couple of these experiences, the pups begin to lick the dam around her mouth when she finishes her own meal, and she vomits in response. Many owners encourage face licking with petting and praise. Then, when the maturing or adult dog jumps up to get a little "love and kisses," he gets scolded or punished. This inconsistency can lead to problems.

Chewing

With the transfer to more substantial food, suckling and licking fade and are replaced with picking up food by lapping with the tongue or grabbing it in the jaws, followed by the swallowing reflex. In the wild, wolves and dogs start earning their nourishment early, between about six and twelve weeks of age. They work for it in the sense that they must do a lot of ripping and chewing at prey animals killed by older pack members. This may serve a dual purpose: priming young noses and taste buds for their natural prey, while developing tremendously strong jaw muscles that eventually will crush many spines for survival. Pet puppies do not experience this chew-for-food stage, but usually gain strong jaws anyway chewing on toys. None of this toy-chewing relates to filling their bellies, so this oral activity becomes a pastime, a sort of hobby. And being great fun, it often gets generalized to the rest of the environment; almost anything becomes fair game; shoes, furniture, carpets. Fortunately, chewing problems are basically related to tension-relieving behavior, so there are ways to minimize the damage. In the meantime, one day dog food may be sold in tough, edible containers that will keep pups and adult dogs busy for a half hour or more, chewing for their chow, rather than gulping it down.

Following Behavior

A fascinating and useful behavior shows up as the pup develops eyesight sharp enough to see things moving at a distance from the litter; he follows them. Just what is moving doesn't seem to matter. It can be a mechanical toy, littermate, his mother, or a person. Even if you isolate a puppy where he can't see any moving things until he is several months old, he will engage in this following response. This important tendency forms a basis for all his later bonds of social development. The response will also be an indispensable part of both the development and correction of behavior problems.

Social Competition

Between four and seven weeks old puppies begin to sort things out socially between one another. This starts with clumsy play fighting, which helps develop coordination and experience about who is strongest and/or more skilled in the physical arts, as well as who gets to the dinner table first. Some pups even try sexually mounting their mates, with no obvious motive other than to be bossy. Most of the biting during this stage is mild and rarely causes any evidence of pain. By the seventh week, however, things start getting serious. Nips get painful, growls become snarls, and fights turn out winners and losers. Losers give up by running away (flight) or showing "freeze" behavior (passive defense response). Winners stalk around picking fights until they get whipped into submissive behavior themselves, meet their equal and declare a truce, or wind up "top dog." Meanwhile, in the loser's bracket, further sorting out takes place to determine where on the social ladder each pup will rank.

The Social Ladder

It is important to understand that puppies, even the most submissive, are capable of acting dominantly, and that the most dominant of them will often display submissive behavior. Which behavior chosen depends on the social circumstances. In an eight-puppy litter, the second-ranked pup will act submissively to number 1 when he approaches dominantly. But later, number 2 will look like a number 1 as he approaches and dominates number 7 in the hierarchy. As the litter matures, these displays are refined into very subtle signals. In the early stages, a dominant dog may have to

Submissive vs. dominant stances.

pounce and pin an underling to prove his point. After a while, merely staring at him can cause a subordinate to lower his tail and head and look away, signaling submission. Another example occurs when the dominant pup approaches, tail up, ears forward and places his muzzle over the subordinate's head or shoulders. The underling may stand still, lower his head and tail, even growl as he raises his lips in a kind of smile. Boss pups learn to recognize and respect this growling and baring of fangs as part of the canine submissive ritual, so long as the other doesn't make a wrong move.

All this ritual keeps domestic puppies from injuring each other while among the litter, which is as far as most of them will mature together. In wolves and wild dogs, however, dominance and submission rituals will determine which animals eat first and get the best and most of the prey, as well as which ones breed. These rituals play important roles in the survival of the fittest and propagation of the species. Not so with our domestic pet dogs. Their matings are either accidental or based on physical conformation. Food is amply provided under noncompetitive conditions. While their wild cousins will mature as cooperating members of functional packs, our pets are usually doomed to lifelong emotional and functional adolescence. They are fed when hungry, supplied with water, washed and groomed when dirty, walked or given outdoor access when needed or asked for, petted and stroked when they nudge for it (or just because we feel they are cute), and given medical attention when required. Since we wait on their every need and respond to nearly every whim, it is no wonder our puppies grow up feeling they are the leaders in our relationships.

Mother's Lessons

Mentally and physically healthy dog mothers are incredibly patient with their offspring. Very much like wolves, they graciously tolerate constant nudging for attention, playful pounces while asleep or drowsing, pups hanging onto tail or ears—-all without responding with punishment. In fact, I have called hundreds of ethical breeders to discover how many have ever witnessed (or seen evidence of) any of their canine mothers shaking their pups by the scruff of the neck. Only one incident was reported, and that was a fourteen-week-old terrier pup who tried to take a fresh beef bone from his mom. Even then, the shake was extremely brief and not vigorous.

Most dog moms simply move away from pestering puppies. If they can't, the harshest treatment is a quick snarl and movement toward the pup with her snout, which is more startling than punishing. If you ever read advice to shake a puppy to punish him, the writer is either ignorant of real life in healthy canine litters, parroting something read somewhere, or lying. I strongly advise owners not to shake pups. Like a human baby, a puppy's optical tract is not fully developed until he approaches five months of age. Shaking a puppy or baby can cause injury to the nervous sytem. As yet, and unfortunately, there has been no research into a "Shaken Puppy Syndrome," as there has been into the problem affecting human babies.

The Critical Seventh Week

The following incident illustrates some of the basic differences between pups relating to littermates versus people. Years ago I demonstrated part of my Puppy Selection Test for CBS-TV. We carefully observed a litter of seven-week-old Golden Retrievers, identifying the dominant litter boss and the lowest ranking pup. As I entered the litter enclosure, the dominant pup led the group to jump up and greet me, while the most submissive, bottom-ranked (also the smallest) pup hung back timidly. I picked up the boss and gently carried him to an area away from the sight and sound of the litter, placed him on the ground, walked away, crouched down and beckoned to him, softly clapping my hands. Cautiously, tail down, he approached me. When he arrived, I gently rolled him onto his back and held him with one hand on his breastbone. He froze. When thirty seconds had passed, I released the puppy and placed him in a sitting position at my feet. The "boss-dog" then proceeded to urinate on my shoe, much to the glee of the TV crew, who were using a close-up lens! I picked up the puppy, praised and petted him during the trip back to the litter. When I placed him down back "home," he immediately started picking on the nearest littermate.

I then took the submissive litter runt away for the same test. Tail up, she resisted my invitation to come, bit at my hand, flailed and scratched when I held her in the submissive rollover, and tried again to bite me when I put her in a sitting position to pet her. This phenomenon, with few exceptions and variations, bears out the contention that puppies do not necessarily perceive persons as they do other dogs, but react uniquely to each. It also shows the difference between rituals of dominance and the ultimate defense reflexes to fight, take flight, or freeze.

Reactions to Threat

A pup or an older dog may react to perceived threats to their physical well-being by acting submissively in an effort to convey the idea, "OK, I give up. Please don't hurt me." If we recognize this and ease off, good. But if we press an already submitting dog with even more severe threats or painful punishment, we violate the rules of the canine dominance/submission ritual. This often creates enough perceived threat to cause the dog to respond to his basic defensive nature. The result may be a pet that is a submissive wetter, a runaway, a fear-biter, or a dangerous, aggressive beast.

Eye Contact

People who stare at other people make them feel uncomfortable. This is true as well throughout the mammal world. Dogs are no exception. This sort of psychological, long-distance bullying can create problems in the basic relationships between owners and their dogs. It can also lead to a dog bite when practiced with aggressive strange dogs. Staring threats invite hostility where friendliness ought to exist.

Training for Fighting

When pups are kept together as a litter through the ninth week or so, serious trouble can break out. Bully-types get more so; mid-rankers vie with greater intensity, and all may turn on an especially submissive puppy and injure or kill him. For these and other reasons yet to be mentioned, it is wise to obtain new puppies

A calm and confident owner begets a calm and confident dog.

between six and eight weeks of age. Observing the litter for about an hour before and during feeding time can be educational. If there is serious aggression between puppies, and you dislike breaking up dog fights, it is a good idea to move on and look at another, more peaceful litter.

This seven-week principle for the transition from canine to human companionship does not mean a behavioral tragedy will occur should you get yours earlier or later. Fortunately, many breeders expose their litters to socialization before, during and after the so-called best age. If this has been the practice, it should be easily recognized when you observe the behavior of older litters.

The Dog in the Human Family

Imitative Behavior

The most important single social characteristic of a pet dog has a Greek tongue-twister for a name: allelomimetic behavior, which literally means behavior that is "of one another imitative." *Allelo* comes from genetics, and *mimetic* was tacked on by pioneers

"Has he been watching an awful lot of TV?"

studying genetics and behavior. The simplest form of this trait common to all social animals can be seen when schools of fish or flocks of flying birds move and change direction as if they were one. Well-socialized litters show it when they all flock happily toward somebody entering the litter area. On the other hand, I have seen unsocialized and poorly socialized litters show fearful, extremely timid, or downright hostile reactions when people entered their domain. The important difference between dogs and other allelomimetic animals is that dogs raised in human families will take their cues from people.

Our pet dogs reinforce our own emotional expressions of happiness and affection; they run when we run, show concern when we are distraught and even share many of our hostilities. Yet, ironically, the very things that create our close social bonds also lead to most of the behavior problems. We cannot ignore the emotional aspect of our pet relationships and expect to understand canine behavior. The causative approach to coping with—or avoiding—problem behavior depends on understanding it.

Investigation

An appealing but trouble-making behavior that begins blossoming at about six weeks of age is to look at, smell, paw at, chew, and taste nearly everything in the environment. At the same age the eyesight of puppies is getting keener almost daily. So it is no wonder they are always in hot water if left alone around the house. This intense investigating recedes with experience, but without proper guidance it can create major problems later. Just as with a human infant, things that might injure puppies should be placed out of reach, while allowing as much investigation as possible. If the pup starts toward a no-no, a quick hand-clap and distraction toward another article or activity should be used. If a puppy must be left alone, it is best to leave him in his regular sleeping area. This will usually cause him to sleep, since you are not there to stimulate activity. Canine playpens are sometimes helpful. They allow plenty of room for spontaneous bursts of activity and those long, crawling stretches after naps.

Fear

As a pup approaches ten weeks of age there is a period wherein certain events can produce lifelong fear responses. Not only that, but other things associated with those fear-producing elements can become conditioned fear-stimulators. This can be used to advantage for teaching a pup to avoid venturing into streets on his own, if the lesson is supervised carefully. But it can produce behavior problems based on unreasonable fears, or phobias, about being left alone.

For instance, a puppy yipped and wailed when left alone in the kitchen or laundry room on his first night in a new home during this fear period. His behavior was absolutely normal, but the new owner wanted to get some sleep. He had read somewhere that "natural" punishment for puppies is to grab them by the scruff of the neck and shake them. The owner didn't recall (if the book or article even mentioned it) how hard to shake, what pup-response to look for, what type of nervous system could or could not tolerate such punishment, or what type of defense reflexes might be most amenable to the shakedown routine. So he just started shaking, and the puppy started screaming bloody murder, another natural response. So he shook harder, which stimulated the pup to higher and louder wailing. Violent shaking finally stifled the puppy, who settled for soft whimpers and sought to get physically close to his new owner. The owner also had read that praise for stopping unwanted behavior was needed. So he picked up and cuddled the pup, told him what a good dog he was, placed him back in his box, closed the door and went to bed for an uninterrupted night's sleep.

If we hark back to the puppy's social, reflexive, and defensive properties, even ignoring the fear-response period, we can see the possible dangers in this type of approach. Some of the subsequent problems are obvious: submissive wetting in the presence of the man who punished him; extreme anxiety when left alone, resulting in tension-relieving, destructive chewing; difficulty in housetraining; and biting the family children when they attempt to correct the dog later in life. The foregoing are not just possibilities. This is based on numerous case histories. More than one night's traumatic encounter was generally involved in producing adult fear-biters. However, this is a classic example of how early mismanagement sows the seeds for problems later.

Sex

At about twelve weeks of age, puppies start going through puberty. They begin sexually mounting both living and inanimate things. If there was ever an area of behavior where projecting human feelings to animals is valid, this is it. The sight of a puppy unabashedly humping away on a blanket or somebody's foot usually stimulates instant, negative human feedback, based on human moral standards of conduct. I have seen both male and female dogs, neutered and intact, with serious aggressive problems, whose owners have either tolerated or encouraged their pet's misdirected amorous behavior. At the other extreme, overly harsh physical punishment has led to the very same type of problems. This paradox might be due to aggressive tendencies that develop at about the same age. What-

"That's what I wanted to ask you about Doctor."

ever may be the cause, the best method for correction is to use the orienting reflex to interrupt the mental fix on the activity and instantly redirect the dog's attention to some play activity, such as chasing a ball. This avoids the excesses of either permissiveness or punishment. If the distract-to-play routine is used, even the most humpy pups hold their sexual expressions in check in short order.

Sleep and Dreaming

From all outward appearances, puppies dream quite a bit. Just like people, their eyes move vigorously in a stage of sleep called Rapid Eye Movement (REM). If you wake a person every time his eyeballs start gyrating, you can cause all sorts of emotional and behavioral abnormalities, including signs of neurosis and psychosis, even hallucinations. Depriving a pup or mature dog of his REM sleep has produced some bizarre canine behavior. In one case the explanation given by the owners was that the pet seemed to be having terrible nightmares and that waking him seemed the humane thing to do. Back when I used to make house calls, I entered the apartment of a young couple whose seven-month-old female Fox Terrier was described as "irrepressibly unruly." Seeing no dog, I asked where she was.

"In the closet," came the unison reply. I suggested we let her out, but the lady said, "Before we do, I want you to know that if you can't help us we're going to have to get rid of her. John hasn't had a good night's rest in five months." John had been waking the dog every time it whined during a dream. In fact, John had been sleeping on the floor with Foxie for the previous three months!

When the closet door was opened, a canine behavioral cyclone hit the room. Foxie jumped up at us, raced around bumping into furniture and walls, barked incessantly and was impossible to control. Before forty-five minutes passed, she wore herself out and went to sleep on the sofa beside me. Whispering, so as not to wake her, I advised John to rejoin his bride in bed at night and stay there. Even if Foxie's dream-state whimpering woke him, let her work it out herself. Five days later he phoned to say what a great dog they had. She even stopped chewing and barking when they left her alone.

The Need to Fight

For most pups there is no need to learn the canine martial arts. However, at around thirteen weeks of age most of them act as if there were. Among other dogs they will engage in exhausting play-fighting sessions. Unless anger sets in, problems don't usually occur. However, when play turns to anger, it is best to break it up by distracting the dogs without getting angry yourself. Scolding or punishing either dog risks conveying the idea that you are taking sides in the dispute, which can increase the chances of far more serious fighting later.

Given no other animals on which to exercise their playful fighting tendencies, most puppies will either invite, or respond to, play-fighting with their two-legged pack members. This can teach a most unfortunate lesson; the pet learns to contest his people

Discriminate between friend and foe.

with physical force, which usually includes his jaws. Worse yet, if the puppy gets angry during the fracas, he has also learned to lose his temper with people and put real meaning into his bites. The possible consequences are clear; either the human fighter backs off or applies more force until the animal shows submission.

Canine horseplay has a role in wild packs, where it seems to help keep the group together. In fact, in many wild and domestic dog play-fights the dominant animal rolls over, allowing a subordinate to take the dominant role. The reason for this exchange isn't clear. Bringing to mind the dog's various sensory capabilities and our limitations, people would probably make poor dog-pack members, and trying to act like one isn't nearly as easy or effective as getting dogs to act like people.

Territorial and Pack Protection

Territorial and group defense behavior also starts showing itself in the early juvenile period. Strangers and known visitors who might formerly have been gleefully welcomed are now often approached cautiously, sometimes aggressively, or even fearfully avoided. These changes could be the result of the pup's improving eyesight which, at about this age, allows him to discriminate at a distance between family folks and outsiders. Lots of people who get dogs with protection in mind are delighted to see their pups bark and show aggression, so they encourage it wholeheartedly. This can be as ill-advised as is the practice of trying to reassure a puppy by petting him and saying things like, "It's OK, Tuffy." Both of these actions positively reinforce the pup's aggressive feelings and behavior at a time when he really needs to be taught to discriminate between friend and foe.

People who do not want an aggressive defender also make a mistake when they scold or punish this behavior. This kind of negative treatment can teach the pup to feel hostile toward visitors. Whatever the pup's behavior, the best way to avoid problems and teach dependable watchdog behavior is to teach through leadership. If it is a friend or non-threatening person coming near, we should show the pup by approaching the person and standing alongside or walking with him or her into the house, paying little or no attention to the dog. This allows the dog to interpret the situation as the owner feels about it. On the other hand, if we are unsure about the visitor's intentions, we should do what comes naturally and act that way. The pup will likely do the same, thereby learning from your example to recognize the contrast between situations calling for wariness or friendliness.

Territorial Marking

While on the subject of pack and territory, the need to brand things with urine or defecation rates some attention, although it develops later on, at five months of age or older. Objectively, domestic dogs don't need a wide hunting territory or to scent-mark stations to scare off competing predators. They also do not need to

Mark of ownership.

roll in rotten carcasses or feces. Even without the need, most pet dogs seem to want to perform one or more of these practices. It is as if the scent of another dog's urine, the approach of another animal, or a feeling of threat or insecurity about the pack or territory arouses the need to lay a brand on things. One way to cause problems such as chasing vehicles and people, dog- and cat-fighting, escaping, running away, excessive yard-barking, household urine and/or defecation marking, and even aggression toward people, is to allow a dog to place his canine "Mark of Zorro" beyond his own legal territory. To do so creates a desire on the dog's part to return and freshen up his scent posts. Unless it can be done routinely, sometimes daily, this can cause frustration. If it is allowed too frequently, the dog may begin defending the territory aggressively. Some dogs will even urinate on their own pack members when they feel a threat to their relationship. This is a way of saying, "You belong to me." This, as well as leaving urine or feces on an owner's pillow or other belongings, may make a dog feel better, but people tend to regard it as downright insulting.

Vocal Behavior

Pups start making noises very shortly after they are born. These are associated with hunger, pain, being too hot or cold, feeling abandoned, or even feeling content. As they move about and mix things up physically, growling, snarling, yipping, and yowling are added to the repertoire. Barking starts at various ages and, when it first occurs, most pups appear perplexed, as if wondering where the noise came from. Depending on the feedback they get, they usually do a lot of barking, or very little. For instance, if they are among a litter that has reasons for lots of barking, most of the individual pups will tend to be "barky." In a human home, barky dogs can create problems. Also, quiet dogs can be made into barkers through innocent reinforcement by people. Howling as an expression of loneliness, or in response to the odor of a distant bitch in heat, is heard most often in breeds from the northern climes. However, once one dog in an area starts it, many others get the urge to join the chorus. Correction or prevention involves distraction followed by soft-spoken direction to another activity.

Leading or Following

With few exceptions, problem dogs and their people are competing for leadership . . . and the dog is usually winning. The owners, backed into an emotional corner, are so attached that they can't take the dog to the pound or veterinarian for euthanasia. The thought of giving him or her away is unbearable. On an intellectual level, the owners have exhausted all the means known to them for correcting their delinquent, and they are reduced to seeking outside guidance. However, even though well in front in the leadership game, the dogs act as if they don't know it. They keep the contest at a near fever pitch, letting everyone know in no uncertain terms from the moment they meet just who is in charge. Here are some examples of how they do this at our facilities.

When the family car is safely stopped in the consultation area, the door opens, and the dog bursts out ahead of everyone. Either that, or he has to be commanded by the owners to stay or he is physically held back. Good-natured bossy dogs approach me and jump up, to tell me to pet them. Nasty ones stalk around, hike a leg on my walnut tree, show me some raised hackles, circle me, or outright charge me to say I'd better not interfere with their "boss" position. When the owners and I head for the office door, guess who's there first? If the owner opens it, the dog barges through.

To illustrate further for the owner, once inside, I ask the owners to get up as if to leave. No degree of human speed can beat Bowser to the door. It requires another command or some unreasonable physical force if the owner is going to score any points in this part of the leadership game. I have seen this so often, with nearly all problem dogs, that it is almost totally predictable. I have seen it in relationships where the dog was extremely submissive to the owner, and others where the dog had ripped up an owner for simply using a threatening tone of voice. Just who is dominant does not seem to be the deciding factor in most dog behavior problems. Rather, who thinks or feels he or she should be leading in the relationship decides the issue.

Unfortunately, when the pet dog assumes the burden of leadership, he must inevitably meet with frustration and suffer the anxieties and tensions that follow. Why? Pet dogs spend most of the time with their people when the folks are home. They use their communication skills to let the family know when to feed them, when to open doors for them and take them for walks (as well as which direction to walk), when to play with them, when to pet them, and sometimes even when to get up in the morning. These are the functions of a leader—letting people know how they are supposed to behave, not through a master/slave approach, but through canine language that most people find endearing.

However, the time comes when the leader dog, feeling responsible for directing the pack members, gets abandoned by them as they go to work or have an evening out. Or the dog's subordinates act as if they should be directing things, such as when visitors arrive, or the first time at obedience class or the veterinarian's clinic. Then, as owners try to change the rules of the game, frustration sets in, the contest usually intensifies and often gets physically rougher, and feelings are hurt on both sides. What might have started out to be an ideal relationship begins to fall apart. The dogs are suffering from what could be called the Frustrated Leadership Syndrome. So they react in ways that relieve their tensions, at least temporarily. These reactions are called "behavior problems," and include destructive chewing, barking, biting, etc. In reality they are just symptoms of that leadership struggle with the owners in daily life. At this point, many owners consider training the dog. While this seems logical, it does not get to the cause of the problem—the frustration the dog is feeling.

Training

Wild and domestic dogs put a lot of stock in ritual. Wolves ritualize their dominant and subordinate relationships with behavioral displays instead of going through the physical hassle of proving things with a fight all the time. So do domestic dogs. Obedience classes can be invaluable in this respect, particularly if a puppy has been taught without a leash to follow its owners, come to them when called, sit when asked (and learn not to get up until

given permission), and to stay. For a pup given a preschool education, an obedience class is a logical place to learn to get along with
life on the end of a leash, especially if puppy classes are available.

However, many dogs with serious behavior problems are great
performers in obedience class. Many are also washouts. In either
case, a simple, daily off-leash ritual in the house in the morning
can be extremely helpful. It should be quick and intense, no longer
than about three minutes. It need not involve more than calling
the pup or older dog to come, sit and stay. Instant praise for each
response and a few seconds' affectionate petting when it's finished
are all that is required.

What does this accomplish? A few minutes of intense "I'm leading, you're following" helps to reaffirm the leader-follower relationship. It gives the animal a sense of having functioned and achieved
approval from his leaders. Everybody old enough in the family
should conduct the simple exercise. I have never seen it correct a
behavior problem on its own, but as part of a larger, total program,
it has been most helpful.

There are several powerful daily rituals between dogs and
owners. One of these is the "dog nudges, owner pets" routine.
When you consult the actual correctional programs later, you will
notice that nearly all of them take advantage of this ritual. However, they require that this problem-producing ritual sequence
undergo a major alteration, as follows:

Dog nudges; owner pleasantly asks for some simple function
(such as sit); dog sits and owner pets. Some very bossy dogs seem
surprised when asked to earn praise and petting. Some even
refuse to comply, move away, and whine or bark in protest. Others
have been known to go away, lie down, and sulk, like a child
denied a dish of ice cream. However, pouting is effective self-therapy. So in either case, if the behavior is ignored, the dogs soon
return and finally get the message that there really is no free
lunch and the group has a new leader!

C H A P T E R 6

The Puppy Primer

If you haven't read the first five chapters yet, save yourself some time and do so—very carefully. Much of the advice here runs counter to the traditional way of bringing a pup into a human household, and knowing the reasons behind it will help you and your new puppy benefit from easier and better ways to raise a canine companion.

Why a Dog?

If you haven't had a discussion among all those who are going to live with the future pet, have one. This can bring up all sorts of sources for human conflict about the dog *before* you get him, especially in families with children.

For instance, many a pup has wound up in the laundry room on his first night because the children got into a fight over whose bedroom he would sleep in. The "Why a Dog" discussion can help gain agreement from everyone on the most important issues in puppy raising. These are:

- Where will the puppy sleep at night?

- Where will he be kept in the daytime?

- What housetraining method will be used?

- Who will feed the puppy?

- Who will clean up the pup's messes?

- Who will take the puppy out for toilet and socializing?

- How will the puppy be taught commands and who will do the teaching?

- If the pup is to be scolded or punished, who will do it and for what reasons?

- Who will bathe, brush, and groom the pup?

- What kind of play will be taught?

- Will he be allowed on furniture?

- Will he be given food tidbits?

These are elements that create family friction and can lead to serious behavior problems if people do not agree and consistently live up to their agreements. It's better to debate them before the puppy arrives than to introduce him into a "war zone."

What Type of Dog?

Big, medium, or small; skinny, heavy, or medium body type; long, medium, or short coat? No matter the breed, these are things that need consideration from a behavioral standpoint.

Here is a list of physical traits that have been the basis for problems, due to human conflicts about them.

Hair or Coat Types

Short hair: The reason it's short is not because it doesn't grow; these dogs shed, all the time. The hair works its way into carpets and upholstery and is extremely hard to extract therefrom.

Medium length, straight hair: These dogs also shed, and many have undercoats that come out in great gobs at regular intervals.

Curly hair, medium and long: These dogs require regular grooming, but some do not shed. Instead, they pick up foxtails, dirt, and debris and shed these around the house. They also may come into the house with bits of feces hanging from their rumps.

"Some people think they're ugly. I think they're appealing!"

Picking your breed may be easy!

Tail and Nose Types

Long tails: They can clear off coffee and end tables. They can hurt when making contact with persons while in full-wag.

Pug-nosed types: Some of them snort a lot, and sometimes their noses emit a spray.

Loose-lipped types: Some of them drool uncontrollably.

These are the physical traits that have created problems, not by themselves but by their effects on the people living with the pets. It is a pity that any dog would find itself banished to the backyard for life or hustled away from visitors because of his physical characteristics. However, it does happen, and can lead to problems.

Size of Dog

Giant Size: They usually get much bigger than people expect. Problems can crop up in cars and in walking on leashes. Visitors are sometimes frightened of them.

Large Size: See Giant Size.

Miniature Size: They are sometimes underfoot when you least expect them. Also, people tend to pick them up a good deal.

Toy Size, Teacup Size: See Miniature Size.

When you have selected your type and breed of dog, make sure everyone has considered the possible negative social reactions they may feel about any of these traits.

Selecting a Puppy

A simple test can help you decide, from among all those cuddly balls of fur, which pup would be best suited to you and your environment.

The idea for the test came to me after so many of my clients said, "I wish you could have seen him in the litter. He was so cute. Who would have thought he'd be such a problem?"

As a matter of fact, I would have! Pups have certain tendencies that begin to emerge as they pass about three and one-half weeks of age. These tendencies, such as dominance, submissiveness, and independence, will be revealed by my test. Once you know them, your decision for *the* puppy can be made with more insight.

Puppy Behavior Test

The first step is to gain the breeder's agreement to the test. Once advised that it is merely a handling procedure, most breeders are delighted that you are going to make special efforts to select the right pup. The best age for testing is between five and seven weeks, but up to twelve weeks is still all right. Assign each pup a letter, to correspond with the score sheet.

When you first see the litter, observe from a distance and try to pick out who is most bossy, most shy, playful, etc. You may be surprised to note how differently they behave when you get them away and alone with you.

With the breeder, select an area about twenty by twenty feet out of sight and earshot of the litter. There must not be any distraction stronger than you in the area.

PUPPY BEHAVIOR TEST

BEHAVIOR CATEGORIES

Social Attraction—Select one:

1. Came readily—tail up—jumped—bit at hands
2. Came readily—tail up—pawed at hands
3. Came readily—tail down
4. Came, hesitant—tail down
5. Did not come at all

Following—Select one:

1. Followed readily—tail up—bit at feet
2. Followed readily—tail up—got underfoot
3. Followed readily—tail down
4. Followed, hesitant—tail down
5. No follow or went away

Restraint Dominance (30 sec.)—Select one:

1. Struggled fiercely—flailed—bit
2. Struggled fiercely—flailed
3. Struggled, then settled
4. No struggle—licked at hands

Social Dominance (30 sec.)—Select one:

1. Jumped—pawed—bit—growled
2. Jumped—pawed
3. Squirmed—licked at hands
4. Rolled over—licked at hands
5. Went and stayed away

Elevation Dominance (30 sec.)—Select one:

1. Struggled fiercely—bit—growled
2. Struggled fiercely
3. Struggled—settled—licked
4. No struggle—licked at hands

Assign each pup a letter (A, B, C, etc.). Circle the code letters scored under teach pup's letter in each test section.

PUPS:	A	B	C	D	E	F	G	H	I	J	K	L	M	N	O	P
SOCIAL ATTRACTION																
1.	dd	dd	dd	dd	dd	dd	dd	dd	dd	dd	dd	dd	dd	dd	dd	dd
2.	d	d	d	d	d	d	d	d	d	d	d	d	d	d	d	d
3.	s	s	s	s	s	s	s	s	s	s	s	s	s	s	s	s
4.	ss	ss	ss	ss	ss	ss	ss	ss	ss	ss	ss	ss	ss	ss	ss	ss
5.	i	i	i	i	i	i	i	i	i	i	i	i	i	i	i	i
FOLLOWING																
1.	dd	dd	dd	dd	dd	dd	dd	dd	dd	dd	dd	dd	dd	dd	dd	dd
2.	d	d	d	d	d	d	d	d	d	d	d	d	d	d	d	d
3.	s	s	s	s	s	s	s	s	s	s	s	s	s	s	s	s
4.	ss	ss	ss	ss	ss	ss	ss	ss	ss	ss	ss	ss	ss	ss	ss	ss
5.	i	i	i	i	i	i	i	i	i	i	i	i	i	i	i	i
RESTRAINT DOMINANCE																
1.	dd	dd	dd	dd	dd	dd	dd	dd	dd	dd	dd	dd	dd	dd	dd	dd
2.	d	d	d	d	d	d	d	d	d	d	d	d	d	d	d	d
3.	s	s	s	s	s	s	s	s	s	s	s	s	s	s	s	s
4.	ss	ss	ss	ss	ss	ss	ss	ss	ss	ss	ss	ss	ss	ss	ss	ss
SOCIAL DOMINANCE																
1.	dd	dd	dd	dd	dd	dd	dd	dd	dd	dd	dd	dd	dd	dd	dd	dd
2.	d	d	d	d	d	d	d	d	d	d	d	d	d	d	d	d
3.	s	s	s	s	s	s	s	s	s	s	s	s	s	s	s	s
4.	ss	ss	ss	ss	ss	ss	ss	ss	ss	ss	ss	ss	ss	ss	ss	ss
5.	i	i	i	i	i	i	i	i	i	i	i	i	i	i	i	i
ELEVATION DOMINANCE																
1.	dd	dd	dd	dd	dd	dd	dd	dd	dd	dd	dd	dd	dd	dd	dd	dd
2.	d	d	d	d	d	d	d	d	d	d	d	d	d	d	d	d
3.	s	s	s	s	s	s	s	s	s	s	s	s	s	s	s	s
4.	ss	ss	ss	ss	ss	ss	ss	ss	ss	ss	ss	ss	ss	ss	ss	ss

TOTALS:

	A	B	C	D	E	F	G	H	I	J	K	L	M	N	O	P
dd's =																
d's =																
s's =																
ss's =																
i's =																

Social Attraction and Following

Pick up the first puppy from the litter and go to the test area. Walk to the center of the area, put the pup down facing you, and walk away, looking back at him as you go. Then crouch down facing the pup and gently clap your hands to attract him to you.

If the pup follows or comes readily, tail up, perhaps jumps on you and even bites at your hands, score him dd, double dominant.

If he comes readily with tail up, but does not bite or jump boldly, score him d.

If he comes, tail not up and sidles a bit as he nears, score a single s for submissive.

If he approaches with extreme shyness, perhaps even rolling over or urinating, give an ss for super-submissive.

This procedure should take about thirty seconds. When finished, stand up and start walking away from the pup. Even if you have to walk in circles, keep walking until the puppy either follows or does not follow.

If he does not follow, score an i for independent.

If he follows and tries to impede your progress and even bites at your feet, score a dd. If he follows, tail up, but does not bite or try to impede progress, give him a d.

If he follows, tail not up, with no attempt to impede you, score an s. If he lags or does not follow, but seems to want to, score an ss.

Restraint Dominance

Restraint dominance is next. Gently roll the puppy onto his back, holding him with only one hand by the chest. Place your thumb and little finger under the pup's armpits to stabilize him. Hold firmly, without causing pain, for thirty seconds.

If the pup fights wildly all the time, even bites at your hand, score a dd. If he fights, but is not wild, score a d.

If he fights, but only for a few seconds and then settles, score an s. If he does not fight at all, give him an ss.

Social Dominance

Now sit the pup in front of you for the social dominance section. Pet him gently on the back of his neck and shoulders.

If he bites at your hands or growls, score a dd. If he merely seems to object, score him a d.

If he seems to enjoy the petting, whether or not he turns his head, score an s. If he licks at your hands, perhaps even rolls over, score an ss.

Elevation Dominance

Elevation dominance is the final test. Make a cradle of your hands under the pup's chest by interlacing your fingers. Lift up the pup so he is balanced in your hands off the floor or ground by about five inches. Hold him there for thirty seconds.

If he struggles fiercely, bites, or growls, score a dd. If he merely struggles all the time, score a d.

If he struggles but settles, score an s. If no struggle at all occurs, score an ss.

Making Your Selection

What the scores indicate:

Two dd's with other d's indicate the pup may not be well suited for infants or older folks and may be difficult to handle. If selected, take him through this test daily until he accepts dominant handling.

Three or more d's, even with a dd, indicate an outgoing, bossy pup. Rough physical handling should be avoided. Conducting this test daily can be beneficial.

Three or more s's indicate a pup that usually fits well in most situations.

Two or more ss's indicate a pup who may be highly submissive, needing lots of praise and gentle handling. Heavy-handedness can ruin this type of puppy.

As you conduct the test and compute the scores, here are some things to keep in mind:

- You are making the preliminary test, but if you still have doubts, have other family members test the puppies also. This gets everyone involved, and you may find some pups who react differently, especially to children.

- Puppies who test i, for independent, in the Attraction, Following, and Dominance sections are not necessarily "bad" as pets. If they are selected, they will tend more than others to be a one-person dog. Even then, especially if they test dd in the dominance sections, they will require regular daily exercise of the test sections or it may be difficult for you to gain a leading, dominant position.

When conducting the test, it is best to have an observer who can see into the area without being apparent to the puppy. Let this person keep the scores. This way, you can run the sequence smoothly, without having to stop and make notes.

Whichever puppy you select, remember that he will change as he matures within your own environment. Extensive testing of puppies that have been selected with this test indicates that between about four and seven months of age the pup may seem to belie his "type." However, as he matures further, he will tend to revert to type. Your greatest advantage in using the test is that you make the final decision after handling each puppy on a one-to-one basis.

With your choice made, it's time for the ride home.

The Ride Home

Riding home in the car may be the puppy's first experience with mechanical monsters, so it's important that it be as pleasant as you can make it. Put the pup on a towel or blanket, beside someone, or on a lap. If the weather is cold, warm up the car; if hot, cool it down, if possible. Cold or heat stress can help create a lifelong carsickness tendency, so try to avoid it.

If the pup vomits, urinates, or defecates, don't fuss. Just clean it up and carry on.

Some puppies naturally start whining, yelping, or wailing. Don't try to punish it out of the little one. Just put a reassuring hand on him and continue homeward.

The Arrival

When you get home, put Mother Nature to work right away on the housetraining program. Take the pup immediately to the spot for his future toilet area. When he performs, do the point-and-praise routine and hope the puppy sniffs his deposit and the general area. If not, just take him into the house so he gets the basic impression that going inside follows performance of his outdoor duties.

When you get inside, let the puppy investigate. If everyone sits around in a circle on the floor, it will give the pup a chance to get to know and identify everyone by smell, since he can't see too well yet. Let everyone interact naturally with the new pet. This is no time to be "walking on eggs" or for criticism of the way anyone is behaving. However, if someone gets nipped too hard, have them roll the nipper over into the restraint dominance position and hold him there until he calms down. Then, release him with praise and pet him according to the social dominance routine.

Have fun until the puppy gets tired, then show him the bed. A blanket in an upturned cardboard carton in which you have cut a doorway has many advantages. It affords the puppy his own place where people can't accidentally drop something or step on him, and most pups enjoy getting into something at sleeping time. This arrangement is also portable, so it can be easily carried from one room to another the first night.

Housetraining

If you follow the housetraining program strictly, you will be amazed at how quickly you have a fastidious puppy. Read it until you can almost recite it, so you don't miss any of the steps, especially with regard to the two important phases involved.

The First Night

You can find all sorts of advice on how to isolate your puppy on the first night in a new home. I will not comment on these, except to say that if you intend to stick your new pet away somewhere alone, brace yourself! Steel yourself against doing *anything* in response to the racket you'll have to endure.

Your puppy probably slept through the night quietly among his littermates the night before, so I have found the best plan is to take the sleeping box into someone's bedroom. Put it right next to the bed, where the puppy can hear the breathing sounds of another living being. Most pups will sleep nicely in this situation, at least until a reasonable hour the next morning, when another opportunity for housetraining occurs.

Socializing

From the time you get a puppy until he is several months old, he needs exposure to and guidance in all the situations you think he will face in life. This includes happy trips in the car to various places, including the veterinarian. Use the Jolly Routine before, during, and after trips to the clinic or hospital. Show him around to all the personnel who may have to handle him one day. This will make everybody happy. Gaining an early, friendly impression with patients forms the basis for a peaceful future relationship for all.

Three trips a week out into the big, wide world will help round out a balanced personality in your dog. These might include visits to airports, the countryside, schools and the like, with opportunities for meeting children, old folks, and other animals. (Ask the doctor about health restrictions that might be necessary.)

Just as going out is important, so is having people into the house to meet the puppy. Make special efforts in this area and you will be able to mold a socially delightful canine companion for life.

These are the vital points involved in selecting and bringing a puppy into the human fold so as to avoid behavior problems. If you already have another dog, or are having a new baby soon, consult the program on "Babies, New Pets, and Dogs." If that old puppy bug-a-boo *chewing* is on your mind, consult that program. When you have digested these first six chapters, you should be on your way to a rewarding future.

Puppy Training

Emotional Development

Training involves our conscious efforts toward teaching. However, your puppy will learn his most important lessons when you are not deliberately training him. These lessons revolve around the pup's emotional reactions to life's new experiences.

91

For example, the pup's first visit to your veterinarian helps shape lifelong responses to treatment. If he whimpers or cries when vaccinated and you act overly sympathetic or upset, *the puppy will get an emotional message* that there really is something to be upset about. On the other hand, if you are calm and happy, the pup will minimize his own behavior and follow your emotional example. This tendency holds true especially when the puppy is between five and thirteen weeks of age. It is vitally important that you expose your puppy to all sorts of people, babies, and other animals during this period so that he will develop a healthy personality. If you take the responsibility for emotionally guiding your puppy, you will help him grow into a well-balanced adult pet.

For instance, when you have to leave your puppy alone and you express concern while leaving, the pup will feel upset because you are upset. While he is alone, the emotional tension builds and problem behavior such as yelping, chewing, or house soiling may occur.

Name Recognition

Out of all the words your dog hears you utter daily, how is he to learn that any particular word is meant for him? The answer is simple: Just say the pet's name before any command word! For example, you name your puppy "Skip." What should "Skip" mean to him? It should mean "Pay attention to me because I am about to say something important to you."

However, if we chat with another person about what Skip did today, the pup soon requires that we change our tone or volume to gain his attention. Here is a tip that can guarantee lifelong instant response by your dog to his name: **Use a nickname when you are talking *about* your puppy, and use his real name when talking *to* him.**

Leader or Follower?

As important as emotional development is, a pup also needs to learn simple commands like come, sit, and stay, if only for his own safety. All dogs are capable of either leading or following. Leader pups become extremely frustrated when they cannot open doors, get their own food, and so forth. A follower is usually a happier dog because he accepts his people's directions.

Test your puppy to see whether he is a leader or follower type. Take him to an open area and walk away from him. Chances are he will follow you. If he does, say "Good dog" and crouch down to attract him to you. If he does not follow you, try running away from him and crouch to praise him if he starts toward you. Try to perform this exercise daily in all sorts of situations from the time the puppy is able to walk.

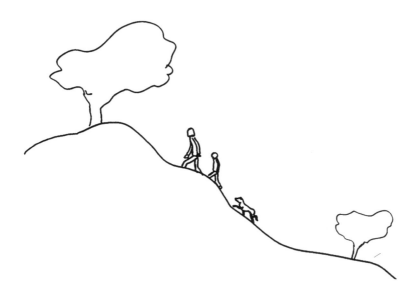

If the puppy does not follow and actually resists following, the following ritual can help achieve a better follower. Gently roll the pup on his back, holding him in that position with one hand on his chest. The puppy may struggle, cry, and otherwise resist the restraint. Calmly persist until the pup quiets down and remains still for a moment. When this happens, release him and give lots of praise and petting. The puppy will soon accept and even begin to enjoy the submissive position. Furthermore, you may notice that he will start following you when you take him out for open air exercise. This rollover is not recommended for pups older than four months.

Teaching the Commands

Teaching Come

Take your pup to an area that is fairly open, but free of strong distractions. Go to the center of the area and watch the puppy closely. The instant he takes his eyes off you, call, "Skip, come!" Immediately crouch down, turn sideways to the puppy, clap your hands, and gleefully praise, "Good dog, good dog, good dog!" Keep up the praise and clapping until Skip comes all the way to you. Pet sincerely but briefly, then stand up and step away *behind* the puppy.

If his attention does not stay on you, instantly call, "Skip, come," again and repeat the entire procedure. If Skip gets distracted, repeat the call and the praising-crouching routine.

Continue until Skip will not leave you no matter where you walk. Then stop that teaching session. Do not hold another for at least two and one-half hours, otherwise you will be overdoing it.

For the second and following sessions, either create more distractions in the first area or go to a new area.

Hold three daily session at the most for six weeks. In between do not use "Skip, come!" unless a panic situation arises wherein life, limb, or property may be in danger. In less serious instances when you need Skip to come to you, merely say "Skip" and then crouch, clap, and praise. These non-emergency times do not require the full "panic" command, and to use it then might wear out the effectiveness of the full command.

Teaching Sit

Sit is the simplest thing to teach a pup. The difficult idea to get across is when to quit sitting! In other words, now that Skip is sitting, how long should he remain so? To communicate the total idea that sit means to sit until I give you permission to get up, proceed by gradually lengthening the duration of the sit.

To achieve the sit portion of the command, first call, "Skip, come!" using the full panic command in an undistracting area. When Skip arrives, pet and praise, keeping your left side toward the pup. Then, as you rise to stand, take your left or right hand and stroke under his chin upward to a spot over his head, so Skip must look upward and backward to keep watching that hand. As you do this, say "Skip, sit."

Praise instantly if Skip keeps looking up at your hand. Lean a bit backward yourself, but do not loom over the dog. If Skip does not sit down, merely repeat "Skip, sit" and again make the over-the-head movement with your hand. The instant he sits, lean down and pet him on the chest and throat, praising verbally as you do.

After about five seconds of sit, say "Free" and step away from Skip to communicate that he can now move out of the sitting position. Crouch down and praise and then keep repeating the entire procedure until sit is achieved on the first command. In this first session ask only for five seconds in the sit. In the next, try for ten seconds and keep doubling it until you have reached approximately five minutes.

If the puppy starts to lie down by your side after longer times have been achieved, do not correct or reprimand at this stage in the process. Remember, first he is learning to sit and remain in that place for some time.

Once sitting for five minutes has been achieved, you may then correct the lying-down behavior by using your hand movement to counter it the instant Skip shows a sign of beginning to lie down. Verbally praise the puppy when he corrects himself, which will be very quickly if you use this method.

Teaching Stay

Once again using movement as the communicator, begin work in nondistracting surroundings with "Skip, come," "Skip, sit." Then say "Stay" as you abruptly bring your left palm from a position about a foot in front of the pup's nose to a spot about one inch from his nose. Stop your hand abruptly.

As he stops, step forward with your right foot (with the pup at your left side, the right foot is less apt to draw Skip forward) and face the puppy. Now you are confronting each other. This tends to keep Skip frozen in this sit-stay. Remain out front for only five seconds and then pivot back to Skip's side. Then, step forward with your left foot and say "Free" and release.

Just as with come and sit, proceed to teach stay in easy steps with minimum distractions at first, then progress to working in different areas and with greater distractions over a period of six weeks.

If Skip starts to break the sit-stay, avoid harsh corrections or manhandling. Just rush back to the exact spot Skip started the sit-stay, call him back and start over. Avoid punishment and negatives to retain your position of positive leadership.

Adopting a Dog

Before you select a dog for your home, this firm commitment must be made: Everyone in the household must agree on which dog to adopt and agree that they will keep him, no matter what. If you adopt an older dog with the idea that you'll "see how it goes," you risk creating behavior problems because the dog has already lost at least one "family," so he already has feelings of social insecurity. When these feelings combine with the dog's ability to sense whether or not you sincerely want him, you can appreciate that the dog could suffer a double dose of insecurity. Also, he may have had behavior problems in a former home. Previous owners rarely mention them because they want to place the pet in a nice home. However, even if there were problems, these won't necessarily carry over to yours, especially if you follow these instructions faithfully.

This adoption program is based on the author's experience, gained from "adopting" hundreds of genuine problem dogs. These pets came to us with all sorts of problems ranging from viciousness and dog-fighting to "incurable" house-soiling. Remarkably, in a couple of days, most of them settled in as if they had arrived as puppies, and the problems either did not erupt in our home, or they were cleared up through the proper BehavioRx correction programs.

Selecting Your Special Dog

Try to select the dog at the home or facility offering him, not at your home. This minimizes stress. If you decide not to adopt, the dog won't become more confused than he already is. Take the whole family along, including any other pets, if possible. If you already have a dog or cat, use the program for "Babies, New Pets, and Dogs." Follow the instructions. Find out everything you can about the dog's medical and behavioral history. If these don't reveal anything problematical, make sure again that everyone is happy about the dog. Once everyone agrees, it's time to head for home. Go to your veterinarian as soon as possible. Have a complete physical done on the dog so that the doctor and staff can get to know your new pet.

The Ride Home

The rule for the trip is: Don't fuss over the dog. Let him settle down in his own time in the part of the car where you intend for him to travel in the future, whether it is in the back seat or the front seat. Expect the dog to be a little "hyper" at first, but don't try to pet or soothe this away or you will reinforce his behavior and anxiety.

Arrival at home is a great time to teach the dog his new toilet area. So take him into the house, give him some water, then immediately take him to the toilet area you want him to use in the future. Stand there quietly, and let him investigate. When he urinates or defecates, go to it and point at the "stuff" and say "Good dog." If the dog comes over and sniffs it, pet him happily and head back for the house and show him where the water bowl is located.

The Need to Investigate

When everyone is in the house again, let the dog go about the house checking things out. Do not follow him, or he might get the idea that he is leader of his new pack, so to speak. Just go about your family business.

The Search for Leadership

One of the first things the new dog will look for after satisfying his curiosity about the physical environment is leadership . . . "Who calls the shots around here?" Depending on past experience with his former owners, he can behave in so many different ways that the only sensible course is to apply the principles of leadership yourself.

Sniffing and checking things out

The first step is to ask the dog to do something in order to gain his "good dogs" and the petting he needs. This is our "no free lunch," learn-to-earn praise and petting program. When he seeks your attention and approval, tell him plesantly, "Tippy, sit." Most adult dogs already know this, so he is quickly retrained. When the dog sits, praise him and pet him briefly and go about whatever you were doing. If he keeps pestering, it gives you a great chance to find out the extent of the commands already known. So tell him to sit, praise and pet him, then tell him "Tippy, down," as you slowly bring your hand, palm up, down through his visual field to a spot in front of his feet on the floor. You'll be amazed how many commands a "new" older dog can learn when he is highly motivated to please. Keep this learn-to-earn routine in place as part of your daily life for at least six weeks.

Feeding

If possible, have some of the same diet the dog has been accustomed to on hand. This avoids loose stools and "accidents" which can arise from abrupt dietary changes. Feed him twice a day to keep something in his stomach most of the time and to avoid hunger tension and the problems that once-a-day feeling can produce.

Sleeping

Don't isolate the dog. Have him sleep in a bedroom where someone is sleeping. The canine social tendency to "be like" their people will result in a good night's rest for all. Expect him to be a

RMM

bit restless the first night. This is normal. The best reassurance you can provide if he gets up to roam about is to call him back to his sleeping place, praise him, and reward him with an affectionate pat or two. Then turn out the light and go to sleep.

Housetraining

You may not need it, but this housetraining routine should be followed as insurance against possible problems.

Phase I: When the dog finished each meal, "shoo" him out good-naturedly, saying, "Toilet" (or some other code word) to the toilet area, ahead of you if possible. Then stand still and let him sniff around for the "preferred" spot. The act of sniffing seems vital as a warm-up to elimination. Do not distract the dog by urging him to perform. When the "duty" is performed, crouch down and point at the urine or fecal matter and say, "Good toilet." Look right at the stuff, not at the dog. If the dog sniffs it, praise and pet him enthusiastically before going back inside. This entire formula should be followed after each meal for adult dogs, and as follows for puppies:

After waking up, even from a nap;

After extreme excitement

After drinking water

After prolonged chewing on a toy, etc.

When he starts to sniff as if looking for a spot to eliminate.

In about four days, the pup or dog should automatically head for the toilet place after meals or whenever the urge strikes. If he takes longer (and he may if your pup or dog is from a pet shop or has been caged before you start this program), be patient. When he seeks a place on his own, you have completed Phase I of the program. He now knows *where* to go!

Teaching When and Where Not to Go

During Phase II of the program, it is vital to keep feeding times as constant as possible. Do not feed at 7:30 a.m. on weekdays, then delay meals on weekends for the sake of a little extra sleep. This ruins the biorhythm of the program and makes the dog anxious.

In Phase II, you do not let him out to the toilet area at times when you are not normally home, such as when you are working. It's impossible to teach your dog to control himself Monday to Friday if you constantly let him out Saturday and Sunday! So, whenever you see signs that he wants to "go" during the taboo hours, clap your hands or snap your fingers to distract him and quietly tell him "Good dog" to take his mind off the urge. This positive program usually succeeds in three or four days. If an accident occurs, this is vital: Don't scold or punish. Just quietly take the dog out of the area so that he doesn't see you cleaning up the mess.

Exercise

Avoid going for walks until about six weeks have passed and your newcomer has settled in for his permanent stay. Tossing a ball or toy for about ten to fifteen minutes a day provides plenty of exercise. The best time for exercise is in the morning. This gives the dog a reason to sleep during the day when you have to leave him alone.

Finally

Congratulations, new dog owner, and good luck . . . you deserve it! Without you, another fine dog may have been lost to humanity.

WHAT CAUSES A DOG TO MISBEHAVE?

How People and the Environment Create Behavior Problems

Unfortunately, a book cannot consult with you and say exactly how you or your environment might be creating your dog's behavior problem. The following thumbnail sketches may, however, be useful in identifying some of these factors. With what you have learned about your dog's reactions, senses, social development, and ways of communicating in Part I of this book, you should be able to identify the causes for your problem, make various adjustments to your environment, select the appropriate correction program, and start on your way to an effective, humane solution.

The Human Element

These profiles of problem people and environments are deliberately exaggerated for dramatic effect. The cartoon humor may help you see more clearly into your situation. I am pictured perfectly as the Domineering-Physical-Verbal type. You may find yourself somewhere, too.

Name-Droppers

Name-Droppers sit around and talk a lot about their dogs, using the pet's name. Then they claim the animal ignores them when they use the same name to get his attention. No wonder. They "trained" the nonresponse. These folks benefit if they give the dog two names; a new one to use for talking about him, and the old one to be used only when speaking to the dog. **Use of the dog's own name should be followed by praise and petting, and used before feeding, and in various other pleasant situations.** Excellent, revitalized response is usually seen within a day.

"Sit, Tippy."

"Down!"

Yo-Yo Makers

Yo-Yo Makers shout "Down!" while quickly raising their hands up away from the dog, which signals up. When Yo-Yo Makers learn to crouch down or reach down to pet the dog before he jumps, most jumping problems are resolved.

Back-Talkers

Back-Talkers usually put the dog's name after a command word (e.g., "Sit, Tippy"), rather than before it, which would let the dog know they are about to command him. When they realize that dogs do not hear backward, they turn things around and begin communicating effectively.

Pointers

Pointers stand rigidly upright with a demanding forefinger aimed at a spot by their side or feet, telling the dog to come. This body language actually communicates, "Stay still, like I am." Worse yet, they may send a message of aggressiveness and/or impending

The Whirling Dervish!

punishment. Pointers are generally amazed at how quickly their pets learn to come when they crouch, clap, and praise.

Whirling Dervishes

Nearly always late leaving for work, Whirling Dervishes race around the house getting ready, winding up their pet's misbehavioral mainspring. When they suddenly disappear, the dog is left to unwind itself without supervision. Many of them chew, bark, or dig at furniture or carpets. Setting the alarm clock five minutes earlier than usual and getting up when it goes off can help correct the dervish situation.

Neat-Freaks

Neat-Freaks make sure that everything is in its proper place, usually just before leaving the house. They go around adjusting throw pillows, and moving books, while the ever-watchful dog takes careful note. When left alone, *the pet mimics the behavior,* continuing the chore. Finding the owner's fresh scent on forbidden articles often makes them too irresistible not to chew on. To solve this problem, most Neat-Freaks have to break their own habits.

The Domineering Physical type.

Domineering–Physical

These types are hands-on people. They push down on their pet's rump, even when the dog knows the word sit. They don't often praise, either. They are also usually Pointers (the human type). This human behavior is usually motivated by the "me master, you slave" attitude. They often become excellent with dogs when they learn to use non-physical treatment. Once enlightened, they often ask, "Does this work with kids, too?"

Domineering–Vocal

The drill-sergeant syndrome is found in people with all sorts of personalities. It comes about most often through failure to reinforce the dog's desirable responses with liberal praise and some quick petting.

Sweet-Talk/Strokers

These attempt to gain the pet's loyalty and obedience through sweet talk and prolonged petting, usually called "fondling." This can create several reactions in the dog, from a desire to mount the owner, to a serious overdependency. Then, when the owner scolds the mounting, or leaves the pet alone, the dog becomes frustrated and anxiety sets in. Misbehavior follows.

Once these owners appreciate that sympathetic tones and prolonged petting "spoil" the dog, a more matter-of-fact tone is usually adopted and the "no free lunch," earned praise, quick-pat technique helps solve the overdependency problem.

Permissives

These want their dog's affection and often give in. They allow things like getting up on the furniture, but don't allow it when guests visit, at which time the pet is scolded or punished. The inconsistency of the relationship frustrates the dog and leads to problems. Depending on the type of dog, the problems range from submissive wetting to viciousness toward the owners and/or guests.

Most permissive owners are very pleasant and easy to get along with among people but often complain privately that others take advantage of their good nature, as do their dogs! After seeing the benefits of using good-natured, but consistent, guidance with their dogs, these owners tell me they have even started saying "No" to unreasonable requests from their family and friends!

Ambivalent Owners

These people suffer from the classic love-hate relationship. That is, they love the dog but hate his behavior. Most are considering getting rid of the pet but say that they "want to do everything possible to solve the problem" before making that fateful decision. Ambivalent types need to realize that dogs sense when their owners are not committed to keeping them no matter what. When this commitment is made, the dog's behavior usually starts improving immediately and total correction follows quickly.

"Paranoid" Pet People

I put "Paranoid" in quotes because it is used here in a lighthearted and inaccurate way. But I have seen pet owners who would swear on the Bible that their dog or cat has it in for them. Most often the pet is seen as getting even or punishing the owner. If spiteful behavior does exist in pets, it must have been learned from people, because wild dogs do not display it. The bad behavior is just another way to release tensions caused by some frustration in their relationship. The solution is to change the supposedly spiteful behavior by removing its cause.

Common-Sense Owners

Common sense leads to sayings like "What goes up must come down." However, new information calls for a closer look at old ideas, since we now know that what goes up may never descend—at least to where it started from. In the world of dog behavior problems there are all sorts of corrections that appear to make common sense. Most of these concern doing something to the dog. For instance, it makes some sort of sense that if you fill a freshly dug hole in the yard with water and then stuff your canine excavator's head into it until he almost passes out, the dog will avoid digging in the area. As a matter of fact, most dogs actually will avoid digging there again. Even more predictably, however, the dog will find somewhere else in the yard to dig. So instead of the problem being solved, it spreads as the dog continues trying to work off that tension.

Another "logical" solution from a Common-Sense owner's point of view concerns the dog's practice of chewing up pillows and the like. This one says that if you stuff the chewed up material in the dog's mouth, tape the mouth shut, and leave it for some time, the dog will not chew that material anymore. This is sensible if you want your dog to avoid things that are already chewed up, such as tattered pillows. However, a little more common sense might bring one to the conclusion that unchewed pillows are what the dog ought to avoid. In the meantime, applying these seemingly logical techniques tears at the fabric of an already stressed relationship between owners and dogs. Frustration mounts, anxieties and tensions become stronger, and problems get worse. Too often, logical owners conclude there is something abnormal about the pet, and get rid of him.

Naive Owners

Naive types have never owned a pet before and usually select one that fits their preformed ideas about how a dog ought to look and behave. When the animal doesn't fit the notion, the owners usually follow everybody's advice, at least for a day or two. They are great book buyers, too. Let's hope this one helps!

Experimenters

These are usually recently married and want to use the pet, generally a dog, as a test animal on which to practice parenting. The trouble with this is that puppies mature to the juvenile level so quickly that the "parents" usually cannot make adjustments in their areas of disagreement between themselves before serious problems start to occur. The best advice for experimenter types is to raise dogs as pets and raise children as children.

Model-Buyers

They are not necessarily naive, but they obtain dogs with the misconception that certain breeds always behave in the same way. This myth is roundly supported and propagated by many dog breeders and the media, especially movies. When the behavior doesn't fit the myth, some Model-Buyers return the dog to the breeder for a trade-in. Some breeders actually take trade-ins.

It is important that Model-Buyers understand that each dog's behavioral development depends a great deal on the owner.

The Jekyll and Hyde Syndrome

We all have our ups and downs. The Jekylls and Hydes show the effects to their dog with gusto. They often leave their problem dog in the morning with apologies and words of consolation usually based on feelings of guilt. This convinces the dog that there really is something wrong with being alone, so he gets anxious and tense. Then, off to work goes kindly Dr. Jekyll. When Jekyll returns home and finds the dog has misbehaved, the diabolical Mr. (Mrs. or Ms.) Hyde roars into action. Ranting, raving, scolding and/or punishing, now convince

"Bye, Bruno, poor lonesome boy! Be good, Bruno, baby! Daddy see you tonight."

"So,! You've been bad again, Bruno!"

the pet that homecomings are also something to worry about. Thereafter, the specter of Hyde's arrival creates enough anxiety for some more tension-relieving misbehavior.

Jekylls and Hydes usually change their behavior when they understand facts about the dog's biological clock, his inability to associate previous misbehavior with delayed punishment, and the need for consistency in human behavior to provide the reliable leadership dogs need.

Problem Environments

Problem Children

Most kids get along well with dogs when the parents provide gentle and enlightened guidance to both. However, when emotional and/or physical parental excesses take place, children and dogs both tend to react according to the "Be-like, act-like" (allelomimetic) principle mentioned earlier. For instance, if an owner gets angry and scolds or punishes a child quite often, the dog may start getting edgy when the youngster is around him. On the other hand, if they do the same to the dog, the child may start trying to play the role of punisher and get into trouble when the pet defends himself. If owners

TABLE 9-1. CHILDREN'S ROLES IN DOG BEHAVIOR PROBLEMS

Child Behavior	*Dog Response*
Pulling ears, tail, hair; sticking fingers in ears, eyes	Growling, snapping, biting
Hitting with hands or objects	Growling, snapping, biting, submissive wetting in pups
Teasing with toys, food; staring, wrestling to the point of anger or rage	Biting, viciousness
Encouraging aggressiveness toward outsiders, other dogs	Biting, viciousness, chasing, dog-fighting, cat killing, killing birds, escaping, barking
Tidbitting with food	Begging, overprotectiveness of food, food-stealing
Playing tug-of-war	Biting, stealing things, chewing
Screaming and/or running	Biting, jumping, chasing
Scolding, punishing	Growling, biting
Being unruly	Being unruly
Inter-child fighting	Aggressiveness, biting, overexcitability
Too much petting	Mounting, aggressiveness, males urinating in house, biting other children

have family problems, the best action is to seek some competent guidance about it while working on the pet's problems.

With that said, there are still some things children do with dogs that can be the basis for mild or serious problems. Table 9-1 lists them. Be sure to keep the "Be-like, act-like" principle in mind while handling them.

My Dog-Your Dog Jealousy

A young married couple had a two-year-old, spayed Doberman with a chewing problem. I always ask clients why they select a certain breed of dog. The answer in this case was protection, which in these times is not unreasonable. The next question was why they got a female. The wife answered, "Oh, Bob picked her, probably because he knew that females like men better than women." Bob's rejoinder was immediate: "Not at all, Martha. I didn't get a male because I was sure you'd spoil him so much that he'd get overprotective of you!" "Well," Martha retorted with a withering stare at Bob, "She's your dog and it's your problem. I just came to this consultation because Bill said it would be helpful." If looks could kill, Bob would have been on his way to the mortuary. Meanwhile the dog began to whine.

I broke the mood, saying, "Since you've put your finger on the problem, let's figure out how to resolve it." With that, we were on our way to working with the "green monster syndrome," jealousy, which is often involved in problems. Jealousy over a dog is tough to work

RMM

out, since it is usually never expressed openly. Bob and Martha were exceptions to the rule. There is a way to bring the green monster out and slay it: Talk about it. But, if things get too hot emotionally, spare the dog. Go out to dinner or take a walk. Discuss hang-ups and agree on how to conduct whatever correction program fits the problem.

War Zones

These are households with two or more people and one or more dogs. The people spend a goodly amount of time firing verbal blasts at one another. These are either low-level holding actions, or full-scale attacks. They are sometimes accompanied by hand-to-hand combat, especially if teenage children are involved. Not all war zones are so evident. Some involve intermittent sniping, which takes the form of verbal zingers, usually aimed at the ego structure of the enemy. In either case, the problem-dog gets into the action one way or another: directly by joining the combat forces through aggressiveness or barking; or indirectly, in ways that vary from chewing to self-mutilation. War zones often require professional mediation but at least warrant a stable truce if the dog's problem is going to be solved.

Hermitages

Hermitages are at the opposite extreme from war zones. Usually occupied by one person and one dog, they can also have several of each. The people don't like outsiders, so the dog never, never gets to find out about them, except for trips to the veterinarian. In extreme cases, house-call veterinarians are used. Under such conditions, active, socially outgoing dogs can develop problems ranging from unruliness to aggressiveness. Calm, submissive types usually do better.

The Fortress Syndrome

The Fortress Syndrome is seen in households where *people distrust nearly everyone*. Owners peek out windows when cars pass or pull up. Every noise is investigated to see if prowlers might be in the yard, or out in the hall if the fortress is an apartment. Fortresses are often established as a reasonable response in high-crime areas. Dogs residing in fortresses can acquire problems of all sorts, but usually bark too much or become overaggressive.

How Health and Nutrition Affect Your Dog

Regular veterinary checkups and routine inoculations may seem to have nothing to do with the behavior of your pet, but dogs and other pets are more likely to develop behavior problems when they have a physical problem. When you feel a nagging pain in your tooth, ear, or stomach, you have the freedom to visit your dentist, otologist, or general physician. Not so with your pet. Unless that nagging pain is accompanied by a swelling or eruption, or hurts so much that the animal cries out, he is doomed to suffer in silence.

Health

Animals can react to physical problems very much like people. They can get irritable and become withdrawn or easily excitable, but they also may start to urinate too much, over or undereat, chew themselves or other things, bark excessively, or exhibit other unusual behavior. The only defense against the behavioral side effects of less-than-good health is a regular examination by the one individual with the qualifications to declare an animal fit—your veterinarian.

During the years I operated a full-time behavioral consulting service for pet owners, it was a policy that clients have their pets examined before starting any course of correction for a problem. This policy sprang from hard experience, not accident. A case illustrates the point.

Hyperkinesis in Dogs

Many clients brought dogs to me that did not appear able to settle down, along with other complaints ranging from biting to housetraining problems. Dealing with the main complaint was hopeless. The dogs, for the most part, were absolutely uncontrollable. Not only were the clients and I unable to control them; the dogs themselves seemed incapable of any self-control. Their every waking hour was spent in activity.

During this time, some extremely important work was being done at Ohio State University's department of biopsychiatry by Samuel Corson, who was working with dogs showing hyperactivity. Through proper veterinary examination, more than 3 percent of my clients' pets were discovered to be hyperkinetic, similar to hyperkinesis in children. After proper medication with *Ritalin* or dextroamphetamine, the behavior of these dogs changed dramatically, making them easy to handle and a pleasure to live with. Where many clients had considered euthanasia, even if privately and with remorse, they instead gained what they called literally "new dogs."

Physical Ailments and Behavior

The results of proper diagnosis and treatment of a hyperactive animal are dramatic but no more vital than diagnosis and treatment of some very common health problems. The following table lists some physical ailments and related problem behaviors.

PHYSICAL PROBLEM	ASSOCIATED BEHAVIOR PROBLEMS
Urinary tract or vaginal infection/inflammation	In-house urination; sexual mounting; self-mutilation; biting; chewing; false pregnancy; digging; barking; masturbation
Anal sac impaction—mild	House-soiling; aggressiveness; self-mutilation; overexcitability; barking; escaping; biting
Pancreatitis	Eating stools; poor learning; self-mutilation; chewing; overeating; house-soiling
Visual problems: cataracts, optic nerve inflammation, brain-related causes and visual/motor complications	Biting; fighting other dogs; aggressiveness; shyness; fear of objects, people, sounds; escaping; running away; chewing; poor learning leading to housetraining problems; self-mutilation
Hip dysplasia	Biting; shyness; self-mutilation; chewing; aggressiveness
Dental problems	Chewing; barking; biting; self-mutilation; digging; poor eating
Ear infections/deafness	Barking; biting; moodiness; chewing; lack of obedience; housetraining problems

While there are many other health problems that affect behavior, these conditions usually go undetected by owners.

It requires years of experience based on proper veterinary education to detect and treat ailments that affect behavior. Seemingly simple problems such as intestinal worms, a condition tolerated all too often by pet owners, can affect functions of the nervous system. The microscopic larvae of certain kinds of pervasive parasites can and do penetrate the brains of dogs and cats. Often there are behavioral changes before we even notice the physical effects of such illnesses. A simple stool sample and regular examination are a pet's only protection against such ravages. However, the dog or cat cannot order it done; it is up to you and me.

Nutrition and Feeding

Your dog is a meat-eating predator by nature. If he were born in the wilderness in a pack of pet dogs gone wild, he would start eating the partially predigested contents of the stomachs of adult pack members as soon as he went off his mother's milk, between five and ten weeks of age. This food would be made up of parts of the animals killed and eaten by the grown-ups. The only vegetables involved would themselves have been predigested by prey. When old enough, he would start learning to kill and eat his own prey, which is a basic canine functional drive that domestication has made obsolete.

During the past fifty years or so, an entirely new nutritional industry has been developing—that of pet food. Before that time, pet dogs ate pretty much what their ancient ancestors ate—leftovers from their human masters' meals. The pet food industry was founded as a means of utilizing (and selling) the waste by-products of the human food industry. For a long time the protein in dog food was largely useless to dogs; that is, it was crude protein, but little of it could be assimilated and utilized. Fortunately, thanks to pressure from numerous nutritional critics, the quality of commercial pet foods appears to be improving. There are now special diets for growth, adulthood, and old age, as well as for special physical conditions such as kidney, heart, and intestinal problems. Genetically based allergies have also generated specialized diets. So things are looking up for the nutritional needs of dogs. In the meantime, however, behavior problems can be created, made worse, or made easier to correct through enlightened nutritional treatment.

If your dog is hyper he may, for example, have a food allergy. Then again, he might need a different balance of dietary protein, carbohydrate, and fat. While some commercial dog foods advertise diets as "high protein," they are rarely more than 30 percent protein, while carbohydrates comprise more than 50 percent of the nutritional value. This is hardly high protein! Many dogs, as with humans, are carbohydrate-sensitive and get hyper from too much grain starch and sugar. Increasing the protein in their diet, along with proper vitamin supplementation, actually calms them.

Many dogs that go through unreasonable mood swings from happy-go-lucky to aggressive are victims of allergies, often to certain foods that affect the function of the thyroid gland. The possible effects of diet on behavior seem limitless. At this time there are more mysteries than solutions. So what should the dog owner with a problem do?

The first step in diagnosing all behavior problems should be a health checkup. Veterinarians now have ways to test for and treat food allergies and hyperkinesis. When these tests prove positive, the treatment is usually convenient and economical. The hyper dog that calms down on a higher-protein or hypoallergenic diet merely needs to continue on that diet with a proper behavior program for a long, happy, well-behaved life.

If you find special diets too expensive, there are economical home-brew recipes available. Your veterinarian can either give them to you or advise where they can be obtained. Once the health of the problem dog has been addressed, the proper behavior program should be put into action and carried out for at least six weeks to ensure a permanent correction.

Nutrient Requirements

You have learned how nutrition can affect your dog's behavior. It is certainly true that dietary needs of a dog are the most misunderstood aspect of pet ownership, bar none. And no wonder. A few generations ago, dogs were fed leftovers from the family table and seemed to thrive. These usually included a little meat, some potatoes, greens, even bits of fresh salad—all the protein, carbohydrate, fat, fiber, minerals, and trace elements a dog needed to remain strong and healthy.

Then came modern food processing and the introduction of canned or otherwise preserved dog and cat foods. Some companies told us our dogs needed meat, while others claimed a balanced supply of protein, carbohydrates, fat, and other nutrients from vegetable sources would keep Fido in fine fettle.

The power of advertising has convinced the vast majority of dog owners that commercial pet foods are more convenient, more appealing, and more satisfying than table scraps, which is probably true.

Nutrition definitely affects behavior.

However, certain problems emerge from the conflict between a dog owner's desire to provide a stable, nutritious diet and the feeling that dogs also need variety to be happy.

This feeling about variety in taste appeal, color, and texture is strictly a projection of human eating habits. The fact of the matter is that dogs thrive on monotony in their diets. They retain better health, live longer, and are emotionally more stable eating the same complete, balanced commercial dog food every day of their lives.

On the other hand, if we occasionally make available some table tidbits, our pets can learn to love variety, too. This is where behavior problems can erupt; the dog may turn up his nose at commercial food or start to beg for people food, much to the dismay of the family at the dinner table, especially when there are guests.

Beggers and Finicky Eaters

If you are plagued by a finicky eater or a begging dog, follow this program and you should clear up the problem within about two weeks:

- Feed your dog his regular diet twice daily.

- If you do feed leftovers, place them in the dog's regular food dish at his regular feeding time and delete the amount of normal food equal to the amount of leftovers. If you can, stop feeding leftovers altogether. The dog will be better off for it.

- Before you sit down to eat, walk to a spot away from the table, but where the dog can see the table, and call the dog. When he arrives there, pet and praise him and tell him to stay. Even if you have to repeat this process many times during the meal, do it until your pet stays at that spot for the entire meal.

- When you have finished your meal, go over and praise the dog again away from the table. This will establish a happy ending for his self-control.

Follow this program until your dog simply goes naturally to his spot and remains there for the entire meal. Before two weeks have passed, even in the most stubborn cases, success should be achieved with this program.

Dietary Behavioral Problems

Obesity

Obesity in dogs can be attributed to one major cause: The pet is receiving too much of the wrong kind of food for his metabolic type and activity level. I have seen littermates proceed through life, one of them eating less than 60 percent of the same type of food as his brother, yet maintaining the same body weight. Each dog's system is unique. A little bit of starch may put weight on one animal, while another may burn rather than store the same starch.

If your pet is fat, consult with your veterinarian on a diet that will suit his individual metabolism, then stick to the diet for at least six weeks before you expect to see any dramatic changes in weight. Even if your dog seems wildly hungry, hold steady to the new diet. If he has been overfed in the past, several weeks must pass before his stomach shrinks to normal size. In the meantime, it is normal for the dog to seem hungry all the time, since his stomach is still feeling unfilled, even though all the required nutrients are going into his system.

Keep in mind that fat dogs are the victims of our mismanagement of their diets. We hold their health and longevity in our hands. This means that any tidbitting must be stopped, in fairness to the pet. A dog of normal weight may outlive an obese pet by as much as 40 percent. A little human self-control can lead to many more years of delightful companionship with a healthy dog.

Food Stealing

Stealing food is as natural to dogs as any of their other more primitive behaviors. Historically, dogs are scavengers. Wild dogs specialize in teaming up to steal carcasses from other predators.

If you are unfortunate enough to have a food stealer, resign yourself to the fact that you will have to take careful precautions to control the problem. You have probably tried most of the traditional punishment and scolding routines, so it is best not to continue with these unsuccessful approaches.

There is one procedure that has worked well in many cases. It avoids physical punishment, but takes advantage of events that dogs may find unpleasant.

First, feed your dog twice a day. Then identify his "pet hate." Once discovered, this is used in association with food placed in spots where your dog may try to steal it. An example best illustrates the system.

A Norwegian Elkhound had the upsetting habit of raiding the hors d'oeuvre tray when the family had guests, the only occasions when food was on the coffee table. This dog's pet hate was getting his nails clipped. The owners were advised to keep the clippers handy. Each time the dog so much as looked toward the tray, they called him to them, near the tray, and pleasantly clipped a toenail. Before they had finished a pawful of nails, the dog actually went to a corner and remained there as if riveted whenever the Lazy Susan was produced!

Another case involved a giant German Shepherd that hated to be bathed. The same routine was followed, except each time food was left around, the bath water was turned on and the dog was called toward the food and then toward the bathroom. One week later, after five such sessions, the owners had the sweetest-smelling, cleanest, non-food-stealing pet in the neighborhood.

Some other "treatments" have used ear and/or eye cleaning, putting on or taking off a collar, even going out on a cold night. Whatever your dog abhors, barring physical punishment, apply it to this system for at least two weeks for results that will be permanent. But remember, you still have to be careful about leaving morsels around when you are not there to oversee the situation.

I never advise putting the dog out of the area in isolation. This risks establishing an association between guests and being cut off from the family. Jealousy of guests, rather than avoidance of food, can result.

During any of the procedures involving food, remain good-natured, optimistic, and be patient with your dog. Behavior changes associated with food are the most difficult to achieve but are well worth the time and effort invested.

Analyzing and Treating the Cause of the Problem

Dogs don't often suffer, in the true sense of the word, from behavior problems; people do. In fact, as a general rule dogs rarely cause behavior problems. Owners are usually the culprits. Further, most so-called dog behavior problems don't even rate serious attention until they make people uncomfortable enough to do something about them. Then, all too often, the logical solution to the problem appears to

131

be to "fix the dog." That is, when the dog is misbehaving, stop it and/or make it do something else. This is the *behavioristic approach*. It runs into difficulties because *it deals with symptoms*, such as the act of barking, *rather than causes*.

Another view considers anxiety to be the cause of the problem behavior. This method treats the anxiety. But it usually ignores the cause of the anxiety.

A third approach considers the total dog and his environment. It views the dog as more than a simple "behavioral model" responding to various stimuli by behaving in wanted or unwanted ways. This method recognizes a pet dog as a four-legged member of a two-legged family, with most of the emotional attachments and involvements of his human companions. It sees unwanted behavior as a way for the dog to relieve the tension created by anxiety which, in turn, is usually caused by frustration in the pet's life. For want of a more descriptive name, I'll call this a *causative approach* to behavior problems.

Deciding Which Approach to Use

To get a clear picture of how these three approaches work, let's analyze an actual case from my files. This is about a dog that barks when left alone. It represents a class of problems which poses the greatest challenge to behaviorists, since the misbehavior occurs when the owner is not at home to make corrections. To make it more interesting, we'll consider you are the dog's owner.

Your pet is a good-natured, medium-sized, spayed female terrier mix, two years old. She is in perfect health. You live alone in an adults-only apartment building and have had the same neighbors since your dog was a puppy. Until recently you and your neighbors all worked the usual five-day week, but then the man next door went on a midnight to 8:00 A.M. shift. You knew your dog barked when you went to work, but nobody complained, so it wasn't a problem. In fact, you felt lucky, because one neighbor had a dog that chewed up carpets when it was left alone. At least your Tippy's barking wasn't destructive. But last night your attitude changed. The landlord knocked on your door with a legal barking-dog complaint from the city's animal regulation department, plus an eviction warning.

Now who has a problem? Several parties, in fact! The neighbor who signed the complaint feels bad about it, but he has to sleep to keep working. The landlord, who dislikes evicting anyone, has to live by the rules, so he gives you the legal month to get the situation resolved, apologizes, and starts mentally preparing a want ad for your apartment. Do you have problems! All sorts of things go around in your head. You are ambivalent about the neighbor, whom you like, but you feel like calling him and saying, "Thanks, Ralph! At least you could've spoken to me about it before you called the law! And by the way, forget about that patio barbecue next Saturday night!" But you get a handle on your emotions and investigate ways to solve the problem and remain in your happy home.

What to do? You call your veterinarian, who recommends that you phone me. I give you a rundown on your alternatives in a framework of possible approaches to a correction and usual results.

There are variations on these approaches, but the theme remains the same—treat the barking behavior and/or the anxiety. Both of these approaches ignore an important fact: what goes on between owners and dogs when they are home together influences how the dogs behave when the owners are away. With this in mind, let's go deeper, applying the principles of pet dog behavior using an approach to your problem that reaches beyond simple barking behavior or anxiety, and looks at what is going on in your day-to-day life with the terrier.

The Causative Approach

What is causing the frustration that creates the anxiety and tension the dog is attempting to relieve by barking? When you uncover the answer to this question, and do something about it, the barking usually stops in an incredibly short time—a couple of days in some cases and as long as six weeks in others. However, there's a catch. *You are the only person who knows what's bugging your dog, and only you can take the steps necessary to correct the situation and make the threat of eviction go away.* So, we make an appointment for an interview at your apartment. At the appointed time, the doorbell rings.

For the moment we'll ignore exactly what is being said in our conversation and describe what physical behavior is occurring. As the doorbell rings, the dog runs to the door ahead of you. You open the door, trying to get your leg between Tippy and me. We exchange greetings while Tippy is jumping up and yipping at both. I reach to pet Tippy, who rolls onto her side. I pet her briefly. You close the door and gesture toward the living room. The dog runs ahead and jumps and yips at me while I sit. You sit on a chair opposite me and call Tippy to you. She ignores you. You stand and start toward us, calling the dog. Tippy rolls onto her side again. You pick her up, return to the chair, and put her down into a sitting position at your feet.

The conversation continues while Tippy whines. You say "No" to her, shaking her by the scruff of her neck. You get up to go to the kitchen to turn on the coffee maker. Tippy races after you. I get out my notepad and make notes. Tippy returns to the room, followed by you. You call Tippy to the chair, tell her to sit, and stroke her. She stays calm as long as you keep stroking, while the conversation continues. When you stop stroking, Tippy whines and gets restless. You stroke again. You get up to go to the kitchen for coffee and cups. There is the same routine, with Tippy following you out, leading you back. For the first half hour I ask questions, and you do most of the talking. Then, I explain my recommendations, writing on a form, showing it to you occasionally. I say you are about to learn the power of nonverbal communication with Tippy. Without speaking a word to the dog, you are about to teach her to stay by your chair while you go to the door to say good-bye to me, without any anxiety or excitement on the dog's part. You say, "Fat chance, Bill." We have a little chuckle and start the leadership routine, which goes as follows.

I start to stir, as if to get ready to leave, and you start to get up. Tippy starts wagging her tail and jumping again at me as I sidle toward the door. You go toward the door and Tippy runs ahead. Both you and I quickly return to our seats. Tippy leaves the door, tentatively, and returns to you, wagging her tail. You pet her briefly (two seconds).

You get up and start toward the door. Tippy rushes ahead; you instantly turn and go back to your seat. Tippy returns to you and you pet her briefly. You again get up and start to the door. Tippy sits at your chair, looking expectantly at you. You return to the chair and quietly praise and pet her briefly. This get up/go-to-door/return-pet routine goes on for fifteen minutes, until finally, you can open and close the door while Tippy remains at the chair.

I then accompany you to the door. Predictably, since she hasn't yet learned to stay away in this situation, Tippy leaves the chair and races ahead. We both quickly return to our chairs; so does Tippy. You pet her briefly. Only five minutes worth of the going/returning is required before Tippy remains at your chair while the door is opened for me to leave. You are able to say your good-byes in peace for the first time in your life in the dog's presence.

I leave you a sheet of instructions for your reference and a time for our next appointment. You return to your chair, a thoughtful expression on your face and the recommendation sheet in your hand. As you sit down, you absentmindedly reach down to start stroking Tippy, but suddenly you withdraw your hand. You smile, realizing you have just modified your own behavior and gained important insights about yourself and Tippy.

Let's peek at my private notepad to see what I wrote when you went to get the coffee. My first notes:

1. Tippy excitable, vocal, good-natured, bossy.

2. Tippy feels leader. Too dependent.

3. Physically dominant-negative vocal.

4. Fondling, too-long petting.

If we review the scenario, it becomes clearer where I got my diagnosis during the first part of the interview. Tippy's center-of-attention behavior during the greeting, her yips, and jumping resulted in note number 1. Tippy's leading into the living room, out of the kitchen, back to the door, and following you to the kitchen formed observation number 2.

Tippy's extremely submissive response to my reaching to pet, your own approach when she did not leave my chair, your loud "No" and scruff-shaking created comment number 3. Your continual stroking to keep Tippy calm accounted for number 4.

Now, on to outline what was said.

In the early part of the interview you told me about your workday and weekend routines. I also wanted to know about early housetraining and behavior problems, especially how you handled them. You gave me good descriptions of your actions and Tippy's reactions. Here is a list of important practices and events, with recommended changes:

Event: You feed Tippy once a day, usually right after coming home in the early evening. This leaves Tippy with an empty stomach most of the day because food stays in her stomach only six to nine hours. Also, cramming a whole day's nutrient bulk into her tummy stretches it. Then, when it empties, it is a gaping emptiness. This creates restlessness in all animals. All Tippy's senses are "hyped." Like a once-a-day-fed zoo lion, she becomes anxious about her next meal.

I recommend: Split food in two; feed morning and evening, with the evening meal at least thirty minutes after the latest homecoming time in your schedule. This avoids the anxiety and "hunger tension" during the day.

Event: You jog with Tippy on weekend mornings but never during the week.

I recommend: Jog with her daily or leave her at home on weekend jogs. Either way provides the consistency Tippy needs.

Event: Before leaving for work, you pick up and cuddle Tippy, reassuring her you'll be back. You then put her down, away from the door, saying "Stay!" Then you hurry out as Tippy rushes to the closing door. This ritual of guilt helps to impress Tippy, emotionally, that "something really is wrong." She cannot understand exactly what is wrong, but she feels anxious and frustrated.

I recommend: Sit quietly for at least five minutes before you leave her. Use the walk-to-door, then return routine, without speaking, in place of "Stay," until Tippy stays away from the door. Then leave, without speaking.

Event: At homecoming you and Tippy have a joyous greeting ritual at the door.

I recommend: This builds too much apprehension during the day for Tippy's excitable nervous system to tolerate. Instead, walk in, say "Hi, Tippy," avoid eye contact, then do your other activities for at least five minutes. You may then greet Tippy, away from the front door area.

Event: Whenever Tippy nudges you for affection, you stroke her until she leaves or stops nudging. This "Tippy nudges/you respond" routine makes her feel she is the leader in your relationship. Also, whenever you get the urge to give her affection, you go to her to pet and cuddle her.

I recommend: She is never expected to do anything to earn praise and petting. Prolonged stroking creates an overdependence on your presence. When you leave, she feels overstressed without her petting machine. Do not withhold affection or petting, but ask her to learn to earn praise and petting. In other words, satisfy some of her need to function for a leader.

This routine has been nicknamed the "no-free-lunch program." It goes like this: Ask Tippy to come or sit when you get the urge to give affection or she asks for it. Then pet her, briefly (less than five seconds), and avoid prolonged stroking. Speak your commands softly, pleasantly.

Event: You taught Tippy to "speak" for food treats but rarely do it except when company is present.

I recommend: Do not tidbit Tippy. It has become tied to barking and can compound your problem. Besides, she is performing for the food, rather than for you.

You follow my advice, but it is tough on you. After all, the very reason you got Tippy was to enjoy those homecomings and all that stroking. It is kind of flattering to have a pet who shows that she doesn't want you to leave her. However, after a few days of your leadership by movement and no-free-lunch procedures, Tippy seems so much calmer and less frustrated; you persevere.

Improvement is seen during the first week and all unreasonable barking is gone by the middle of the second week. Two further complaints by the neighbor were due to Tippy's barking when salespeople rang your doorbell, which the law allows. You followed my advice and got a "Day sleeper: Do Not Disturb" sign for your door.

By the way, you did get together with your formerly unhappy neighbor for that barbecue. And Tippy didn't even beg for tidbits!

Techniques to Avoid

Techniques I **do not** consider appropriate in solving dog behavior problems are:

Electrical Shock Devices

Even with fancy labels such as "hi-tech" and "electrical stimulation," shocking a pet dog to control unwanted behavior is a quick-fix method that is totally out of step with enlightened, humane approaches. It can also lead to aggression, displacement behavior problems, and ustable behavior.

Cages

I have never found caging necessary. I also never recommend putting a dog outdoors, in garages, bedrooms, or closets as a means of "psychological" punishment for misbehavior.

Rough Handling

Shaking, hitting, or roughly pressing a dog into submission are not necessary to gain leadership. This type of correction has the possibility of causing unwanted side effects, such as submissive wetting or biting. It can even injury a puppy's nervous system.

Other physical measures that I do *not* recommend are "kneeing" your dog in the chest, stepping on his toes, throwing the dog on his back to stop jumping, or submerging the dog's head in a water-filled, freshly dug hole, until the animal goes limp to correct digging.

These heavy-handed measures are more likely to damage your relationship with your pet than solve problem behavior.

Food Rewards

Food rewards are potent motivators, but fail to address the *causes* of unwanted behavior. Remember Tippy's case!

CORRECTING BEHAVIOR PROBLEMS

INTRODUCTION TO SECTION III

RMM's engaging cartoons are the only thing that will keep you from falling asleep in fifteen minutes if you try to read this section as if it were a "book." There is a lot of repetition because the basis for correcting so many problems involves some of the same basic procedures. However, I did not want to leave out any of the elements, because you will be referring to the individual program as you go through it with your pet.

Read the correction program for your problem as if you were going to have to take an oral examination on it. That way you will commit it to memory and put every element to work. Each correction program has been used successfully by hundreds of thousands of dog owners, who have received pamphlet versions of these programs through their veterinarians (*BehavioRx Series,* by William Campbell). With patience and optimism, you can have a pet that adds joy to your life.

CHAPTER 12

Aggression Toward Owners

This program deals with outright biting and emerging aggression shown by growling. Though the text uses the term "biting," you can substitute the word "growl" if your pet has not yet bitten, but appears on the verge of it.

The reasons for bites or growls may involve anything from overprotectiveness of food, toys, and other articles, to a response to scolding or punishment. Simply adapt the principles to your situation, since the same correction routine applies to all these problems.

When your own dog helps itself to some of your flesh, this is the ultimate insult. If ever I have heard a classic description of "ambivalence," it comes from bite victims. "I wanted to kill that so-and-so, but I was shocked and my feelings were hurt to the quick," is the usual kind of statement. Also, most people say they aren't sure they can trust or feel the same warmth and affection for their pet ever again. The meaning of the statement "Once bitten, twice shy" becomes painfully clear. It is extremely difficult to behave toward the dog with the same confidence as before. The dog senses this change and may take advantage of it, depending on the circumstances that led to the bite.

To start rehabilitating your relationship in a way that will also rebuild your confidence and allow you to correct the problem, you'll have to analyze what type of biting occurred.

Reasonable versus Unreasonable Biting

All biting can probably be classified as defensive, in that it results from the dog feeling threatened. For instance, if you were bitten while applying some physical punishment, it's simple to deduce that the biting was defensive. On the other hand, if you were merely telling the dog to get off the couch, using no threatening gestures, it is hard to say that the bite was defensive. However, in the couch situation, it was the dog's "status" (its feeling of dominance over you) that was threatened. In either case, the basic program for correction follows the same course.

141

"Can you give him something to relax his jaws?"

It is not unreasonable for a dog that feels he is the "boss" of his people to growl at, or even bite, his underlings if human underlings want to pet the boss dog. Extremely bossy dogs tell their people when and for how long they are permitted to pet them, not vice versa. Therefore, even though it may seem unreasonable, touching such a dog, even affectionately, when he is not in the mood, threatens his dominant status.

This kind of dog, basically a leader, dominant and/or independent type, can be classified as "spoiled rotten." We'll call his biting "reasonable," at least to the dog!

The genuinely "unreasonable" biter seems to suffer episodes of insanity. It might be better to say that people suffer from his brief episodes, since some of these dogs, after biting with apparently vicious intent, wag their tails, act submissively, and literally lick the wounds they inflicted a few moments before.

These pets require a great deal more medical attention than their owners usually afford them. They should be given complete physical and neurologic examinations. If the dog is a purebred, the breeder should make a contribution to the cost, especially for a genetic chromosomal analysis. I find that many unreasonable biters suffer from arthritis, hip dysplasia, thyroid dysfunction (usually low), hormone imbalances, hydrocephalus (too much brain fluid pressure), cataracts, prediabetic and diabetic conditions, or even foxtails (grass awns) in the ears. If it is your fate to have such a dog, I hope you will consider medical examination as a reasonable approach to unreasonable behavior.

If your dog bites an infant or child under the age of about six but has not shown aggression to adults or other family children, your best bet is to follow the programs for Biting (chapter 15) and for Babies, New Pets, and Dogs (chapter 13) which apply to such situations. This program is for family members old enough to understand its content and/or carry it out with parental supervision every step of the way.

Don't Punish

Physical punishment must be avoided if this program is to be effective. If your biter bit in reaction to physical punishment, this should seem obvious. On the other hand, if the dog was punished after some biting incident and biting is still a problem, the message must be the same: Do not use it.

The same holds true for "psychological" punishment, such as putting the dog outside. If this practice has not succeeded to date, it probably never will.

The program also assumes you have tried the "shame on you" and "bad dog" routines with no improvement in the behavior problem. So scolding must also be avoided.

The Hyperkinetic Biter

Hyperkinetic dogs, like their child counterparts, are constantly on the move, always seeking attention. They are four-legged response mechanisms looking for a stimulus. I have even seen them bump into chairs, just to get the feedback of the chair's movement! When hyperkinetics also bite, they are usually deemed "psychotic" because their total behavior seems unreasonable.

Physically they may appear normal, but most of those I have met have slightly enlarged pupils, even on bright, sunny days. Compared to normal dogs, they drink very little water. When held in mild restraint their heart and breathing rates go sky high. Some of them salivate a great deal, but they usually swallow their saliva.

It is important not to confuse a hyperexcitable dog with a genuine hyperkinetic. Hyperexcitable dogs overreact to activities around them. Hyperkinetics do not need activities around them; they are always on the move, making things happen around them.

Many hyperkinetics respond well to a medication that would make a normal dog (or child) hyperactive. Instead, genuine hyperkinetics calm down dramatically and appear to become normal. Often the hyperkinetic biter ceases to show any hostile behavior. If this occurs, the dog can be worked through a program of biting correction and will respond even more quickly than the nonhyperkinetic biter.

Both the medical and behavioral programs for correction in these cases need veterinary supervision and guidance. However, they are well worth the time and effort required.

Corrective Program

Social Distance

To change your relationship with your biting dog, you must put some "social distance" between you and him. This does not mean physical distance. Rather, it means that interactions between you and your dog should be unemotional. To accomplish this, all you need to do is take care of the dog's physical needs. This should involve the following, and no more:

- Feed him on a twice-a-day schedule.

- Keep his water bowl full.

- Let him outside or take him out for toilet duties only. If you have been taking him for walks, suspend them until later in the program.

- Avoid all eye contact with the dog.

- Do not speak to the dog, except when absolutely necessary.

- Avoid physical contact with him, except as required for his well-being. For instance, if the dog comes over and leans on you, or gets onto the furniture, merely move away in a neutral manner.

These steps avoid emotional interchange between you and the dog, and set the stage for a revised relationship. This shows itself in many ways. The dog may increasingly try to get your attention, or he may even "pout" for a couple of days. If he tries the pouting routine, let him, and wait until he starts soliciting your attention for petting or praise.

This cooling-off period allows you to assess your own feelings about both the biting incident and the dog. When you feel the dog is trying to warm up to you, and when you feel confident in renewing your emotional and physical relationship (petting, not punishing), the time is usually right to start reestablishing a proper social standing with your pet—one in which you are the leader. This usually takes two to four days.

Determining the Subproblem and Earning Leadership

Getting bitten by your own dog usually happens because of some other behavior problem. If this is the case, consult the appropriate problem program (Chewing, chapter 18; Jumping, chapter 25; Barking, chapter 14; etc.) and follow that program *in conjunction with this one.*

If your pet is to recognize you as his leader, you must function as a leader. Tell the dog to do something, such as "Tippy, sit," each time he asks for your attention and/or petting. If the dog is already sitting, tell him to lie down. Briefly praise and pet happily for obedience. Do not ask him to sit for dinner or breakfast or tidbits of food. You want the dog functioning for you, not for food. Besides, "the hand that feeds" has already been bitten!

If you were bitten in a situation such as when telling the dog to get off the furniture or while handling the dog, you need to understand that the dog bit to put you in "underling" status.

When You've Got "IT"

"IT" is having control over your dog's feelings, as well as his behavior. You can tell by the dog's reactions to your praise, after he responds to the command sit or down.

You won't have "IT" if, instead of sitting, the dog starts jumping on you or moves away, or if he barks or pouts, which may happen with extremely bossy dogs.

You will have "IT" when you see your pet's emotional energy and attention directed to what you want, rather than what he wants. When you feel you have this control, you can start the correction program for the other behavior problem, if there was one that led to the biting in the first place.

Applying the Jolly Routine

What I refer to as the "Jolly Routine" is simply a method of conditioning your dog with distraction. You must recreate, or be vigilant to take advantage of the problem situation should it be one that is difficult to arrange such as coming home and finding the dog on the furniture.

The instant the dog notices you and is in the situation, clap your hands and say anything that will cause the dog to wag his tail. You know what phrases "turn on" your dog, so use them. Some examples are:

"Good dog, Tippy. Let's get the ball!"

"Good dog, Tippy. Wanna go out?"

As you say the good-time phrase, move away from the dog and toward the ball, the door, and so forth. Get the dog to follow you. Do not approach the dog. If he follows, play with the ball or follow through on the activity that started the routine.

If the dog bit in a semidark situation, follow the jolly phrase by turning on adequate light as you move away and attract the dog out of the situation.

If possible, go through the Jolly Routine a couple of times a day, but do not repeat it more than twice in a single situation. Its impact can be diluted if overdone. Besides, the new emotional reactions need time to incubate for the dog to be able to retain them.

If you follow the principles involved in the cooling-off period, and apply the leadership and jolly phases with confidence, you should be back on an even keel with your dog after six weeks. In the event you do not seem to be getting anywhere with this program, you could benefit from the services of an experienced dog behavior consultant.

REMEMBER:

Never create a situation or go into a session unless you feel you have control over the dog's mood. If you feel shaky, your heart is in your mouth, or your pulse is pounding, return to the "Earning Leadership" phase until you have settled down and feel confident again. Always keep in mind that with an extremely bossy dog you must make leadership the hallmark of your life-long relationship.

C H A P T E R   1 3

Babies, New Pets, and Dogs

The introduction of a new baby or animal into the household of an established dog requires some thoughtful preparation. If the established pet is normal, healthy, and well-adjusted, the joy of the occasion should be reflected in his behavior—good-natured curiosity about the newcomer. There are, however, several steps that ought to be taken to ensure an emotionally upbeat tone to the proceedings.

Preparing the Pet

Analyze the relationships between everyone in the household and the pet. Are they positive? Are the people in the family praising and petting for good behavior? What negative aspects are there in the relationships? If there is more negative than positive, then turn this around and work on the problems. An example will help explain this.

A young couple expecting a baby had a small terrier which they had allowed on the furniture when he was a puppy, but then decided to keep off the sofa and chairs. Though they had tried all sorts of measures, including punishment, the dog would jump onto the sofa when the owners were away. This brought about a situation where the dog was scolded almost daily when the owners arrived home to find it just getting off the furniture, or found telltale dog hair thereon. However, both husband and wife admitted they sometimes weakened and allowed the dog up with them, but only on special occasions in the evenings. Otherwise the relationships were excellent among them. With the coming of the new baby, though, they decided this practice should be stopped for hygienic reasons. They felt the dog might have fleas or be a carrier of some disease that could be transmitted to the child.

When the newborn baby was brought home, the terrier, quite normally, was extremely curious about it, wanting to jump up, sniff, and investigate. The parents scolded the dog and put him out of the house. The result was that the dog, a male, started urinating in the house, especially in the baby's room if the door was left open. The

147

problem became worse when the dog was punished after the urine marks were found. Within a couple of weeks the usually happy dog started skulking whenever the baby was present and would not come near it. The owners became worried enough to seek professional advice.

The situation in this case appeared obvious when viewed from outside: Jealousy resulted from an association by the dog between the arrival of the baby and the disapproval, even rejection, by his cherished owners. The solution also seemed obvious but required a change in the attitudes of the owners. The baby's pediatrician agreed that if the parents were worried about fleas and disease, the answer was to keep both dog and household flea-free. A trip to the veterinarian ensured the proper procedure was followed to get rid of any fleas and assured the parents of the animal's excellent health. This included a regular schedule of bathing for the terrier.

Besides these measures, the owners followed a program of praising the pet each time they brought the baby around or paid attention to it. They taught the dog to sit by the sofa, and held the child so the terrier could smell it—all done with happy, praising words for the situation. The result was that the pet soon wagged his tail whenever the baby got attention, since it now was a shared, totally positive attention. The urination problem disappeared overnight.

This case highlights one of the major concerns about newcomers, whether babies, animals, or guests. The best procedure is to make the arrival a happy one that includes the established pet. Better yet, the arrival should mean the animal gets more, rather than less, attention than before. This is why important steps to prepare the pet are necessary.

How Much Attention?

Your pet is highly sensitive to the amount and nature of attention you give him. In preparing for the newcomer, take stock of how much, and at what times you are giving attention to the established pet. For instance, if you feed him at 8:00 A.M. and 6:00 P.M. and the schedule will have to be delayed when the newcomer arrives, adjust the feeding time at least four days before that occasion. This avoids any association between the arrival and the delayed feedings.

If you feel you pay constant attention to your pet, especially if he demands it, cut down on the amount of attention a couple of weeks before the new arrival. However, do not cut down on the positive quality of the attention you give the animal. If anything, intensify it; make him more happy.

If you spend a good deal of time absentmindedly petting your dog or cat, remember that the animal will sorely miss this if he cannot continue when the newcomer appears. Jealousy could result, and problems crop up.

One of the best ways to prepare a pet that constantly demands petting is to teach him to do something for the petting, such as sit. This is a fairly simple exercise that most dogs already know how to perform and it can be used anytime. **The plan is simply to ask for a sit each time the animal seeks petting. Rather than prolonged stroking, make it a brisk, upbeat, brief petting. Then, go on with some other activity.** This will be especially necessary after a new baby arrives. Preparing the pet for it in this way avoids the possibility of the established animal's association between newcomer and any deprivation.

Personal Contact

How closely should a pet and new baby be allowed contact? This should be discussed with the pediatrician. The doctor knows your child, his state of health, and immunization schedule. On the other hand, your veterinarian knows the state of your pet's health. A thorough examination a few days before the arrival should be scheduled. At that time any possible problems can be discussed with your pet's doctor. Thereafter, it is a matter of personal preference. Many parents are comfortable allowing their pets to enjoy extremely close contact with their babies, even sniffing and licking them. Others are more reserved. The plan that works best is one which ensures that the pet does not see the newcomer as an interloper. Rather, the interpretation should be that the newcomer means more positive attention than before the arrival. This avoids jealousy and problems.

Use Your Judgment

You are more sensitive to your pet than any outsider who offers advice. If you feel uncomfortable about introducing a new baby or another pet into the household, so will your pet. This is because your dog probably has more emotional empathy (feels as you feel) with you than with any other being in his life. Therefore, if you feel that the dog is not safe around babies, do not expose the baby to situations which might be dangerous. However, avoid making your pet feel left out. For instance, if yours is an outside dog, intensify your contact with him outside. Do not let the dog feel abandoned after the newcomer arrives. Instead, make him feel he is getting more and better attention.

When Babies Crawl and Walk

Maturing babies not only look different when they start to move about, they also undergo changes in body chemistry and smell different, especially to animals. The first time your baby starts crawling, the dog might be quite surprised. He may want to investigate the baby more closely, might show casual interest, or even be startled and act upset about it. At this time it is up to you to show the pet how to interpret the baby's new-found mobility. Appear happy about the situation, and chances are the dog will feel likewise.

When the baby starts to crawl or walk toward the dog, follow the Jolly Routine. If the dog appears edgy about the baby's approach, happily praise him. Avoid scolding and do not grab the baby away. This can make the dog feel that the baby needs punishing or that something is genuinely wrong with the situation.

Just as dogs like to investigate babies, there comes a time when babies want to investigate dogs. It is not wise to leave babies and dogs in an unsupervised situation where the baby might inadvertently hurt or corner the animal. Unfortunately, babies usually want to poke their fingers into the dog's ears and eyes, which is understandably upsetting to the pet.

Babies do not walk; they toddle. A dog cornered by an approaching toddler, may feel threatened and defend itself by escaping, growling (which the baby does not understand), or snapping. Therefore, it is good practice to supervise the early interactions between nearly mobile babies and your dog. Show your pet a happy interpretation for the baby's activities, and a better lifelong relationship will result.

C H A P T E R   1 4

Barking

If you have a problem barker, there is often more than one kind of "noise" bothering you: the dog's yapping and the neighbors' complaining. When neighbors complain, the dog usually barks when you are away. Either way, a twofold program is called for: The barking itself must be curtailed directly, and the cause for the barking must be removed. Any other problems involved must also be corrected.

Ironically, thousands of "yard dog" barkers are corrected easily by making a simple change—leave them inside the house! Most yard barkers are either not housetrained or are destructive if left inside. If this is your case, it is easier to deal with the inside problem than the outside barking. If the dog has matured since he was banned, try leaving him inside for short periods for a few days. Then, lengthen the time over a week or so. You may find that simple maturity has cleared up the house problem, and your barking problem will be solved as well.

Getting at the Causes

Why do dogs bark constantly anyway? Experience indicates that most bark either at some person, animal, or object, or about some condition, such as being isolated from people or other dogs. It is normal for dogs to bark at animals and people entering or passing by the property. Some city and county laws define this as "reasonable" barking. However, when the barking becomes a problem, you need to understand why and how it started in order to correct it humanely.

Puppies Need Barking Guidance

Most excessive barking stems from early, unconscious training by dog owners themselves. That is, when the puppy first shows signs of territorial defense, the owners are delighted and may even urge him to carry on. But the wisest way to manage a barking puppy is to call him to you, then quietly investigate the situation. You show the pup, through your behavior, how he should behave. Of course, if something is really amiss, the pup will start barking again and you can investigate. This simple approach trains a dependable watchdog.

153

Are You Barking, Too?

Another way to create a barker is to bark back at the dog—outshout him! This often works when you are at home, but all the dog really learns is that you are boss-barker. Thereafter, when you are gone, he takes control and the barking erupts with renewed gusto.

The Solution for All Ages

When the dog starts to bark in your presence, call him to you as quietly as the barking will allow. If the barking is about something unusual that you think needs attention, go investigate, but do so quietly. "Shush" the dog with a whisper if he starts to bark again. Then go back and settle down. Call the dog and keep him close by. Be persistent with this routine for six weeks. During the course of this exercise, you will notice that the dog will sound his first alarm bark, then look to you. If you are out of the room, he will seek you. That's ideal watchdog behavior!

Problem = Barking Dog

Solution   **Usual outcome**

When dog starts to bark, teach it to lie down; dogs can't bark while lying down.

Not so. Dog either learns to bark while prone, or waits until you're gone to bark.

Shout at dog to stop barking; scold or punish.

Dog stops barking when you shout, scold or punish. Waits until you've gone to start again.

Problem = Barking Dog
(continued)

Solution   **Usual Outcome**

Muzzle the dog.   Muffled barking, thirsty dog.

Strap on an electric shock collar; "zap" dog when it barks.

May stop barking when collar is on, but heightens anxiety and dog may substitute other behavior, such as chewing furniture, self.

Surgically remove dog's vocal cords.

Dog screams, may start barking again if cords grow back.

Problem = Barking Dog
(continued)

Treat anxiety by getting dog to sit quietly before you leave it, instead of acting anxious, excitable. Give it a delicious tidbit as reward.

Fat, barking dog.

Treat anxiety by giving dog tranquilizer, sleeping pill, or other medication.

Calm, or sleepy, barking dog, Sometimes stops barking, but drugs have long-term adverse side-effects. Barking recurs when drug withdrawn.

Corrections When You're Not Home

When you are not at home, corrections are more complicated. Territorial barks, as mentioned earlier, are natural for dogs and are part of their functional makeup. However, the dog that makes a full-time job of it in response to normal, everyday happenings needs to be taught other functions to replace his territorial needs. Therefore, part of the correction is to get your pet to function for you rather than the self-satisfaction of guarding his territory.

Learn-to-Earn Praise and Pets

First you need to gain the dog's response to you. Your dog's need for approval as a member of the family group is the key. Therefore, whenever the dog nudges for petting and attention, ask him to sit before petting and praising, then release him from the sit. This is the learn-to-earn praise and petting program, often dubbed the "no free lunch." Everyone in the household must follow the plan. It teaches the dog to function to earn petting, praise, and approval.

All fondling (prolonged petting) must be stopped or the program won't succeed. This is a sacrifice, but the barking problem usually involves a bossy, spoiled dog. And unearned stroking spoils many dogs, especially barkers. After following the earned praise and petting exercise and the dog is sitting willingly, you are ready to make setups to correct barking that occurs when you are not at home.

The Sherlock Holmes Stage—Fact-Finding

First, some detective work is needed. When does the dog bark? Is it right after you leave home? If so, leave a few minutes earlier than usual and use the corrections to be detailed later. Does the barking occur just before, or at the time you arrive home? Then you will need to make arrangements to get home a few minutes earlier than normal for a few days.

In either of these situations you may need someone's help if you cannot vary your schedule. Just be sure the person helping you completely understands the following corrections.

Sneak 'n Peek Corrections

This correction is called "sneak 'n peek." Use the setups by leaving or coming home earlier than your usual time on work days as well as on your days off. Make all your usual preparations for going to work, then:

1. Sit down quietly for at least five minutes in the area that you usually leave the dog.
2. Pay no attention to him. Don't even make eye contact or speak.
3. Get up and leave without a word.
4. Start the car and drive off down the street—do whatever makes the dog think you are really gone!
5. Then sneak back to an area adjacent to the dog, but out of his sight and scenting ability (if outside, stay downwind). The instant the dog displays any sign that he may start barking, such as pacing or whining, or if he does start barking, apply a noise as a "distracter." The distracter must be some sound other than your voice. The sounds must be quick—less than a second in duration—in order to be successful. A single rap on the window, door, fence, etc., interrupts the dog's attention from the barking but avoids revealing where the distracter came from. If possible, make your observation point behind the dog when his attention is on his usual target. When the barking stops, do not praise the dog. Remain silent and repeat the distracter if the barking starts again or if you see or hear the dog getting ready to bark.
6. Continue this routine until the dog settles down. This may take between a few minutes to an hour, but it must be done.

If you must leave for work before total success is achieved, don't worry—complete correction will take a little longer, but eventually you will win. You will know you are making headway when the following happens: A sound occurs that used to cause barking; the dog alerts to it but settles down or just whines or sniffs in the direction of the sound.

Your Patience—A Key Element

If the entire program is applied for a period of six weeks, you should be the owner of a dependable watchdog that does not bark at unimportant incidentals, but that will sound the alarm when there is a genuine threat to you or your property. The sneak 'n peek part of the program may succeed in only a few sessions, but keep up the entire learn-to-earn routine for six weeks.

> Be consistent and patient with your dog.
> The reward will be a peaceful life for all concerned—
> you, the neighbors, and the dog.

Biting

Biting non-family members is the single most serious problem in dogs. This kind of aggression takes time to develop; so, when the causes are discovered, successful treatment will also take time. Practical, professional clinical experience has shown that dogs require behavioral guidance for at least six weeks to achieve a lasting correction. Afterward, certain changes in the environment will probably have to be continued to avoid recurrence. Good-natured, happy, tail-wagging dogs respond most quickly. On the other hand, reserved dogs that never, or rarely, wag their tails, even when you act happy, require more time and care. However, there is hope, even for dogs that may seem incorrigible.

Get the Facts

The first step is fact finding. We must understand why the dog bit. Was he frightened? Of so, of what? Did he feel threatened? What was being threatened? His territory, his group or family member, his physical safety, his dominant status over people?

Develop a History

As a first step, think back to the very first time the dog ever displayed either bossy or fearful behavior, even as a puppy. How did you react? If he was fearful, did you try to be reassuring and pet him? If so, your actions probably told the dog that there really was something to be worried about.

Scolding or punishment is another mistake, because the dog associates the negative treatment with the people, so he blames them for the punishment! Thereafter the dog may become fearful or even vicious when these or other people visit or approach them.

Bite Victims

Some people are prone to getting bitten. Find out how many times the victim has been bitten before and by how many dogs. Unwittingly, these oft-bitten people show fear or hostility, either of which upsets some dogs; some stand stock still, which threatens an impending attack to dogs, especially from strangers. Another type of victim "keeps an eye" on the dog—yet another threat. Staring is aggressively dominant; it challenges the dog to be aggressive.

Some people approach dogs face-on, too quickly, or even grab them by the neck or head to get a kiss. Children, particularly, often scream hysterically around dogs, which can trigger chasing and biting. Other bite victims blow in the dog's ear or tease him.

In all these situations, with the exception of people who tease, biting dogs must be shown how to enjoy these experiences with people; meanwhile, the victims must learn new behavior around dogs. In the teaser's case, we recommend that you explain the situation to them. If they do not change, put the dog in another area at least thirty minutes before they arrive. This avoids any association between visitors and being put out.

Defensive Dog Behavior

Dogs have different types of defense reflexes. When a dog feels threatened he reacts in one of three ways: toward the threat, away from it, or freezing. Fight, flight, or freeze. These reactions occur only when the dog feels extremely threatened. Many dogs seem to belie their real basic defensive reflex reactions. For instance, some dogs are vicious to outsiders but are submissive to the family even if severely punished by them. Dogs at the other extreme bite only family members and are submissive to outsiders.

Almost all dog bites occur because of how the dog feels about various situations. Emotions, not intelligence, probably make up 98 percent of our interactions with our dogs. Emotional reactions trigger biting. So training the dog to respond to commands, while helpful, fails to deal with the cause of the emotional problem.

A Word about Growling

If you physically punish or scold harshly, you should realize that many dogs growl and even show their teeth as a sign of submission. In dog-talk they are saying, "Okay, but please don't hurt or injure me. I may have to defend my life." Just like kids, some dogs give in but grumble about it. If your dog growls in these circumstances, don't increase your threat. Just relax and leave the dog when he stops the grumbles. Then use this positive program to correct your problem.

Learn-to-Earn Praise

Most dogs get petted whenever they ask for it, which gives them the notion that they are the leaders. Turn this picture around; every time the dog nudges for petting, whenever you get the urge to pet, before you open a door, put the food down, etc., pleasantly tell the dog, "(Name), sit" before you praise and pet. Pet briefly on the throat and chest. Have the dog sit until you release him with a word like "free." Extend the length of time during the sit until you reach at least two minutes before the release.

This simple learn-to-earn exercise makes the dog function for you to gain praise and petting. It is the foundation for your leadership position, the basis of your power to change the dog's feelings about things that cause biting. When you feel you have achieved control and the dog is looking to you for permission to go outdoors, eat meals, etc., you can design setups for the next step.

The Jolly Routine

The exercise for achieving new emotional reactions in threatening circumstances is called the "Jolly Routine." You need to take your dog into the situations that trigger his feelings of threat. At that instant, clap your hands once as a distraction, then immediately do something that gets a happy response: Bounce a ball, laugh and act happy yourself, speak a phrase that causes tail wagging, jingle car keys, etc. This exercise switches the dog's emotional response from fear or hostility to happiness. The exercise must be repeated until the dog shows the happy behavior without having to use the Jolly Routine. If your dog never wags his tail or acts happy, you must create some "key" for his Jolly Routine before proceeding.

Events that trigger feelings of aggression or fear might be the doorbell, footsteps on the walk, the sight of a child or adult, etc. Perhaps the dog's first response is barking, running to the door, whining, any outward signs of anxiety. After you gain a jolly reaction to that trigger event, take the dog, by careful steps, further into the situation until the dog is happy from the beginning to the end. Then make further setups involving different people and situ-

---

Warning: If you don't feel confident using the Jolly Routine with the dog off-leash, then use one, but don't let the dog pull on it. Don't risk communicating your tensions to the dog. It can make things worse—not better. If you use the leash, make sure you are standing beside the dog's head or beside the person who is helping you. If you can't use the leash properly, find a competent, humane trainer who will teach you to do so. Do not carry out this program until you feel competent and confident.

---

ations, until the dog, and you, are comfortable in all situations.

As mentioned, it is important to stand beside people. This way, the dog perceives you as on that individual's side, in favor of that person. When you face people, the dog sees you as confronting them, against them. The same body language applies between the dog and others, too. Many dogs relax if people simply turn a side toward them, a friendly signal. Most dogs are reassured if people crouch down sideways. Take the time to analyze your dog's reactions to all of these situations, then use the effective ones in your program.

The Principles

Here are the principles of the correction program:

All family members discuss the history to discover the original causes for the problem.

Put the dog on the learn-to-earn program.

Avoid fondling, because it makes biting dogs jealous about their family relationships and resentful when other people come around and interrupt this selfish relationship.

Find the key to the Jolly Routine for your pet and apply it the instant the trigger stimulus occurs.

Carefully go step by step through the biting situations until rehabilitation is complete.

Nippy Puppies

Finally, let's discuss puppies and their tendency to bite or be mouthy with people. First, avoid tug-of-war. Don't ever tease puppies because it teaches them to use their jaws and teeth on people! To correct the nippy pup, when he starts to nip or mouth, pick him up by cradling with both hands under the belly and chest and hold him with paws off the floor until he settles down. Then gently put him down, praise him, and pet him. Use this elevation dominance exercise at least five times a day, whether or not the puppy shows signs of aggression or nipping.

Don't ever hit or shake the pup, because a basic defensive bite reflex is hooked up to the body, neck, and head, particularly the snout. Therefore, hitting or grabbing these areas stimulates more biting! Also, shaking can injure a pup's visual nervous system.

Patience, Consistency

The secret to success with dogs of all ages is consistency. Be patient, and don't expect instant results. Biting is solved by informed, consistent, humane treatment of the dog by you.

P.S. If you have considered neutering your pet, talk to your veterinarian and follow the advice strictly.

Car Sickness

To appreciate fully the problem of car sickness we have to project to the dog some human sensations. Dogs suffer motion sickness in the same situations as people do, and they respond well to medical and behavioral therapy. This program for car sickness has helped thousands of dog owners who have followed it. It can help you and your pet as well.

Know the Cause

There are several causes for car sickness. One is created when a new puppy, already upset about being taken from his litter, is further upset by the car ride to his new home. If the puppy tends toward motion sickness, he will probably start salivating and then vomit. If the new owners then make too big a fuss over the puppy, pour on too much sympathy, or otherwise get upset, he senses that something is genuinely wrong, and the seeds are thus sown for future car sickness.

The way puppy owners react to situations provides a model for the way the pup will react. I call this the interpretive factor, and it is usually more important than the fact that the puppy got sick in the first place. It is far better to ignore the car sickness than to overreact emotionally, no matter how sympathetic we may feel.

Puppies that have been handled very little often suffer from car sickness. In dogs and people there is an area of the brain called the vestibular center that integrates many of the sensory impressions we receive. It is especially important in the condition of visual, tactile (touch), and balance functions. In very young animals this brain center needs to be stimulated if proper sensory integration is to develop.

Dogs that get carsick often lack this early handling and stimulation. There has been little experience of getting picked up, turned about, and cuddled upside down. Later, these dogs may tend to be car sickness victims. This is not to suggest that if you have a carsick six-month-old big dog you should start hoisting him up as part of your correction program. But if you have a pup or small breed it might be helpful if you do it gently a couple of times a day.

Visual causes are also akin to human experience. Many children who are forced to sit in the back seat get carsick. So do many dogs. However, if they sit in the front seat they are fine. It appears that when the vision to the front is restricted, as in the back seat, the objects seen whizzing by out of the side windows have the effect of causing nausea.

The last cause to be considered also has a parallel in people. Some dogs that are bossy, leader types get upset when they cannot control many of life's situations. And the car certainly puts them out of any position to control. So, like the bossy child, they get emotionally upset and carsick.

The Corrective Program

The first step, no matter what the cause, is to make sure the pet feels you are a competent leader. To do this, ask him to do something each time before you pet him. This can be as simple as telling the dog to sit, then petting him with lots of praise. This will transmit the message (after a few days) that you expect him to earn his praise and petting. Do not curtail your petting, but just ask for some function to be performed before you pet. It is difficult to teach your dog not to be carsick if you cannot get him to function in other ways for you.

Small Beginnings

Take the dog in the front seat of the car for an extremely short ride twice daily, just down the block and back. While getting into the car and all during the ride you must be jolly, acting as if something good is going to happen. If your pet has a favorite ball, toy, or bone, take that along and use it to sustain a happy frame of mind. Follow this routine a couple of times a day for four days in a row, if possible. Also, do it at different times of day and at night. In this way you are teaching your pet in short, happy rides that the car is a pleasant place to be in. If the dog gets sick, ignore him for the time being and do not clean up until you are back home and the dog cannot see you doing it.

When the short rides no longer produce any signs of nausea, lengthen the time and distance of the rides. Do this by five-minute segments. When you reach twenty minutes per ride you then must vary the routes you take. Try a main highway, a hilly or curved road, all the while keeping up the jollity and happy behavior.

Help from Friends

When the longer rides fail to produce nausea, have the dog ride in the back seat of the car. If your pet resists, take along another family member or friend. Warn them against coddling the dog, but have them do the Jolly Routine.

When you have reached this point the program should be carried on for six weeks with at least one car ride every other day to reach permanent success. If there is any backsliding, merely start again with the short rides and you should get things in hand within a few days.

Some dogs have special quirks relative to the direction you take them. If you find this with your dog, do not avoid going in that direction; just proceed at first for shorter distances that way. I recall a Poodle that got ill every time the car traveled in the direction of the groomer! The program of shortened rides in that direction works well in such cases.

If your dog has been on medication for car sickness, discuss with your veterinarian the method by which to wean him off the drug. Sometimes a "cold-turkey" approach works well. However, the doctor knows your dog, and the medical directions must be strictly adhered to for success.

A word about using food rewards to correct car sickness. I have found it to be disruptive. After all, it is the digestive system we need to calm down, and food only tends to excite it.

Follow this program for as long as it takes to solve the problem, which might be six weeks or as short as a few days. Your reward should be a pet that is a joy in the car.

Chasing Cars and Boundary Training

Most of the dogs that become bona fide vehicle chasers have extremely sensitive reflexes to chase anything that moves suddenly or quickly. If your dog has ever "caught" an auto, motorcycle, or truck, you know the serious danger involved for both the animal and the victim. The risk of injury to both parties is frightening and can be expensive. This program is designed to help you overcome the problem of chasing, and running away from the yard, as well as to advise you of the legal dangers involved.

Most communities have leash laws. Check with your authorities. Get a full explanation of the penalties and risks assumed when a dog is allowed to run freely. The consequences have led to financial ruin for some owners. With this in mind, through no fault of your own,

"He chases cars, and the other day he caught a Datsun and simply ruined it!"

your dog may get the urge to chase or run off. This program is no guarantee, but it has helped dogs control the urge, sometimes to the point of ignoring former chase objects.

Establish Leadership

Most dogs that chase cars do so to fend off "invaders" of their territories. Others just seem to make a game of the activity. In either case, the dog needs to follow the example of a different behavior, provided by a teacher. That leadership must come from you and others who live with the pet. The following program must be adhered to strictly if the problem is to be solved.

Corrective Program

Your dog must learn to earn his praise and petting. To do this, you will need to ask the dog to do something when he wants petting and when you want to pet him. For instance, if the dog approaches you happily, ask for sit and then pet him. This little procedure will start to take effect in a few days or less. You will see the dog looking more to you for directions. When this occurs, you are ready to move to the next step in the program. If this does not occur and you do not start to feel you are in control, it may be advisable to find an obedience instructor who will teach your whole family the techniques of gaining leadership. Be sure to find one who agrees to involve all people living with the dog. Having only one person in the household with the ability to teach and lead the dog will not suffice.

Remove Causes for Chasing

There are several activities that make a chaser worse than need be. These must be removed from the environment before undertaking the program.

Walks: If it has been your habit to walk the dog around the neighborhood, this must be stopped before you start this program.

Urination: If the dog urinates beyond his line of boundary, this also must cease. Otherwise, the dog is extending his territory beyond his rightful boundaries and will continue to view cars as invaders.

Fence worrying: If your dog has a fence along which he chases or runs, special steps must be taken to keep him out of that area.

Keep Within Boundaries

The first step to correct a chaser or runner is to establish reasonable boundaries across which your pet should not stray. Wherever this is—the sidewalk, curb, or fence—take the dog (on a leash, for safety's sake) toward that boundary, walking briskly. When within three or four feet of him, shout some word of alarm ("Watch out!") and abruptly turn around and run back toward the house or other area you want the dog to retreat to. Repeat the process until, when you approach the boundary, the dog stops and looks back, or toward you. Be sure to praise the dog each time as you carry out this procedure.

Warning: If cars, bikes, or runners are involved, make sure you have the situation secure; that is, do not run the risk of having a stranger at the wheel of the car or on a bike. Set up with people who are aware of the problem and will cooperate by stopping their vehicle if the dog breaks loose. Put a twenty-foot extension of cord on the leash to allow you to run back toward the safety area ahead of the dog in the initial stages. Never undertake the procedure when risk of injury might be involved.

The Final Test

When the dog no longer shows interest in chasing beyond his boundaries, the next step is to walk with him deliberately beyond the boundaries in the area where chasing has occurred in the past. Make the same type of setup with friends as at the boundary lines, but instead of running back to the home area, simply back away with the same suddenness as before and ask your dog to sit. Keep this up until the dog sits without your command. When this point is reached, continue the exercise about three times per week for six weeks. Do it in different areas until you are sure the dog is responding without your cues to back up and sit. When this happens, your pet has internalized the correction and you can take walks again.

Chewing

If your pet is chewing up things, chances are you have already tried most of the standard remedies such as scolding, spanking, and shaking the dog, but without success. One of the worst things about punishment methods is that they tend to create a breach in your relationship with your pet. The program you are about to put into action avoids physical punishment and will actually strengthen the bond between you and your puppy or older dog.

Puppies usually chew for the same reason human babies chew— to experience the taste and texture of the environment through the oral senses, and to teethe. This is normal developmental behavior for both species. The trouble is, pups have razor-sharp little teeth, which can do more damage than babies' teeth. The pup and older dog deserve the same safety precautions as the baby; put all valuable or dangerous things out of reach. Then give your pet something he will enjoy chewing. Flavored nylon bones, hard rubber balls, and safe squeaky toys are good.

Thousands of case histories have persuaded me to avoid giving things like socks to problem chewers. Dogs cannot differentiate old socks from new socks, or sock materials from sofa material. Young or old, it is best not to tempt them.

To avoid making your pet mouthy, it is a good idea to treat tug-of-war like the plague! It can mouth-orient the animal, so when he misses you he will seek to chew things that remind him of you. Also, tug-of-war places your dog in fierce competition via his jaws and teeth with you, whom he is supposed to respect. I have seen many badly bitten dog owners who indulged in tug-of-war. Avoid it!

Corrective Program

One trouble with chewing problems is that the crime usually occurs when we are not there to correct it. Fortunately, it is what we do when we are at home with our pets that influences how they behave when we are not at home. Most of my clients find that hard to accept, until they follow this program and experience the joy of coming home to an unscathed household.

Before you leave your dog, do not spend the final minutes in a flurry of activity, such as putting things out of reach. Such behavior "wires" the pet for the hours he will spend alone. Instead, sit quietly in the area where you will leave him for at least five minutes, ignoring the dog. Then calmly get up and leave without so much as a word. You thereby set an example for your pet that is serene and unconcerned. If you speak and try to lighten the guilt we all feel about having to leave our dogs alone, you make the animal feel something is wrong. When this highly emotional message is conveyed, tension can start to build. Dogs are great tension relievers; they often chew away all their tensions!

When you come home just reverse the procedure; ignore the dog for five minutes and then greet him, away from the area in which he has chewed up things in the past.

Don't Spoil

Now to the step that is probably the most difficult to practice. If you did not have a problem dog I would not recommend this. But the problem is there and, until solved, you must do this: Avoid all fondling! This is not to say that you must not pet your dog, only that you refrain from the absentminded stroke, stroke, stroke that all dog owners enjoy so much. The reason for this sacrifice is important to understand in chewing as well as in other problems.

If we spend a good deal of time idly petting our dogs, imagine how lonely, abandoned, and frustrated they must feel when we are away. The contrast between our presence and absence is too great. Tension results. And that tension will be relieved, very often, by chewing up things that either smell of or symbolically represent us. Most of my clients say their dogs are spiteful and get even for being left alone when they chew. I tend, from experience, to think the dogs are missing their people and chew to relieve tensions.

Petting Teaches

What sort of petting is permitted in the program? The best kind. The type that helps to create a better-adjusted, happier, more loyal, and enjoyable pet, no matter what his age. When you feel like petting your dog or when he asks for petting, simply ask him to sit, and then praise and pet him. This method gets your dog to do something to earn his pets. If you and everyone else in the household will follow this advice, all will gain a strong position of leadership with your pet. In turn, this creates a more relaxed and enjoyable dog.

Punishment Is Counterproductive

At about this point many of my clients ask me, "What about letting the dog know that chewing is bad behavior? What if I come home and find something ruined?"

Good questions, but most people who ask have already tried in vain to teach the idea that "chewing is wrong" by scolding (or worse). Also, going through all the antics and emotional upset of punishment only teaches the dog to become uptight when homecoming time approaches. And that can lead to even more problem behavior. Besides, the object is not to teach the avoidance of already chewed-up things, but to avoid chewing intact articles.

Here is what to do when you find things in a mess at homecoming. Ignore it. That's right. Pay no attention to it in the dog's presence. Instead, in as calm a manner as you can, take your errant pet out of the area to a place where he cannot see or hear you fussing about or cleaning up the mess.

If you get emotional and handle the articles in the pet's presence, you actually might be practicing behavior-reinforcement. You probably have seen some children who misbehave to gain attention, even punishment. I have seen the same thing over the years in dogs. So, as unnatural as it seems, ignore the mess and follow these instructions. Grit your teeth, and you will soon see the rewards.

Don't let him see you cleaning up the mess.

Protecting Your Possessions

So far we have covered the causes for destructive chewing, how to minimize the effects and remove the causes, and how to avoid reinforcing bad behavior. Now let us consider one negative treatment that is useful only if applied along with the total program.

Remember, it is futile to try to teach a dog to avoid things already chewed up. However, it is helpful to teach him to avoid unchewed, intact articles. This is the only negative system I ever advise, and to be effective it must be applied as directed.

About thirty minutes before you are to leave the dog, take some Listerine mouthwash and lightly daub it on things you want your pet to avoid chewing. That's right, most dogs dislike the taste! Do not allow the dog to witness you applying the stuff. Follow this routine for four days and then stop, only repeating it if the dog backslides and chews things that have been treated.

If Listerine doesn't work, lightly spray unscented underarm deodorant on the items and areas not to be chewed. The first day of this routine, and only on that first day, take your pet out of the treated area just before leaving him. Put some Listerine or deodorant on your thumb and lightly daub it across the dog's nostrils, only on the outside surface. This usually produces a distasteful expression. If it does happen, say "Good dog," so as to reinforce the negative reaction. If you do not get any reaction, do not worry. Repeat this process if backsliding occurs. Of course, if you have that rare pet that likes the taste, abandon the procedure at once!

If you follow this total program for six weeks you should achieve a solution to your chewing pup or older dog. Just be patient and remember that most chewing takes time to develop into a problem. Therefore, give some time for a complete correction.

A final comment regarding bones. If you want to leave a raw beef bone for your dog to chew, ask your veterinarian about the practice and follow the advice strictly.

The Logician's approach to chewing.

C H A P T E R   1 9

Coprophagia

Eating stools, unpleasant as it may seem, is not all that rare and not always abnormal dog behavior. The mother with new puppies eats their waste to keep the litter sanitary. I have seen famished stray dogs eating stools, probably for their slight food value.

Nature of the Problem

Some dogs eat their own stools because their digestive systems lack certain required elements, so they turn to their stools for the nutrients therein. This creates a vicious cycle. In these situations, carefully supervised veterinary guidance is required. The doctor's advice must be followed strictly or else the problem can persist for the pet's lifetime.

Another type of stool eating occurs with puppies. Human children often investigate their feces, and so do pups. Parents communicate their disgust of this practice through words, tone of voice, and facial expressions. With puppies and even adult dogs such communication is limited. The dog can seldom be "taught" to find stools revolting. Once we recognize this, the problem can be dealt with intelligently and effectively.

Dogs who practice coprophagy fall into two types: those who do it at every opportunity, and those who do it only occasionally.

Dogs who eat their stools only now and then need special supervision, both in diet and toilet routine. I have seen hundreds of such cases where the stool eating happens only after the pet is given some extra or different type of food. Their systems cannot handle the new or excess nutrient, and so pass it underdigested. Since the stool then contains nutrition, it is eaten.

Corrective Program

Feeding Program

In all types of coprophagia, the diet must be consistent, both in quantity and content. Any changes can produce loose stools and ruin the corrective program.

The quantity of food required by dogs per pound of body weight can vary so widely as to seem unbelievable. I have seen German Shepherd littermates about the same weight, one of which required one-third less of the same food per day than his brother! The clients felt that their light eater must have either physical or psychological problems. Neither was true. In fact, the light eater outlived his littermate by fifteen months.

Feeding Frequency

Another necessity involves the frequency of feeding. You will have to feed your dog twice daily to succeed, probably for the rest of his life. Dogs hold food in their stomachs about seven to nine hours after eating before it is passed into the intestines. Most of them have a natural cycle time (from eating to eliminating) of about nineteen hours. Our domestic pets usually learn to control this elimination time for twenty-four hours due to the human daily living schedule. This is a desirable situation, especially in cases of coprophagy. Since you have to be on hand to feed the dog, you then are also there to supervise his toilet duties as part of your program.

Watch Stools

The standard used for the amount to be fed is this: Feed just enough to produce a formed, firm stool. If the stool is loose or has a rope-like consistency, the amount fed should be reduced 10 percent at two-day intervals until a formed, firm consistency is achieved. Do not fear apparent underfeeding of your coprophagic. If he begins to lose weight, consult your veterinarian. If your dog is overweight, this program may add years to his life and solve the coprophagia as well!

Avoid Punishment

If you have already tried scolding, or punishing, or rushing to pick up the stool before your dog could eat it, you may be in the predicament where the dog will no longer eliminate in your presence. If this is the case, you will have to get the dog out to his toilet area and then remain nearby as unobtrusively as possible. If the pet still will not eliminate, find some spot from which you can monitor the situation but be out of the dog's sight. Be patient until the dog does his duties.

In all coprophagia cases, after the pet finishes eliminating you must instantly introduce some highly distracting, enjoyable type of activity to take his mind off the stool. This might be bouncing a ball, tossing a favorite toy, offering a car ride, a walk, even just running happily about the area.

Whichever it may be for your pet, use it with enthusiasm. Then leave the area with your dog, praising him all the way so as to reinforce his forgetfulness regarding his stool. After a few such successful distractions, your dog will leave the stool upon finishing his elimination, with no need for your intervention. When this happens be sure to praise him happily as you both depart the area.

Secret Cleanup

During the program and afterward, do not clean up the toilet area when the dog might watch you doing so. Dogs are clever at imitating our actions. I have seen cases of coprophagia wherein this element actually caused the problem; the dog was merely getting rid of the stool, but using a most undesirable method! It is necessary to keep the toilet area cleaned up between uses in this program, but do not let the dog see you.

I am often asked about what type of food to feed the dog that practices coprophagy. The best answer is to feed what the dog thrives on, but make sure the veterinarian agrees with the selection. The doctor knows your pet's metabolic type. Some dogs thrive on relatively high fat diets, others cannot metabolize them. If the doctor prescribes diet supplements, follow the dose requirements exactly, otherwise the program may fail.

Stay with this program for six weeks, and you should experience the pleasure of a dependable pet that will be a delightful member of the family.

CHAPTER 20

Digging

An excellent approach to the problem of the digging dog is the same that a reporter takes when gathering facts for a story. The what, who, where, and when have to be documented as a first step. Then the why becomes apparent.

What, is simple: The dog is digging. That also seems to solve the who. But I often find that not only is the dog involved, but other animals and even people are part of the problem.

Why Dogs Dig

If your dog is digging to escape from the yard to chase after or socialize with other animals or people, and if you have tried to secure the yard, you will have to consider ways to change your pet's environment to solve the problem. Ask yourself these questions:

- When does he dig?

- Is it only when left alone out there?

- If so, why do you leave him outside?

- Is it to avoid some other misbehavior inside the house?

Perhaps it would be simpler to get a dog door or to deal with the inside problem. These alternatives deserve consideration, along with the following program.

Our pet dogs are born and raised in the intensely social environment of their litters. They are "groupies." This early life is the basis for the enjoyment we gain from our pets, as well as the problems. Some dogs cope with social isolation quite well; to others it appears to be unbearable. Those that cannot bear it often literally dig for freedom and social contacts. When these dogs are left outdoors where they can see, hear, or smell people and other animals, it is no wonder that they try to get out to meet them. In many of these cases a dog door or simply leaving the dog indoors solves the digging nicely.

Another element can be the owner who enjoys gardening. The dog is a great imitator. If he watches people digging in the garden he often takes up the practice. This can be stopped when people are home, but not when the pet is left alone. Therefore, a digging dog must not be allowed to witness gardening as a part of his correction program.

IMITATIVE DIGGING

1.

2.

RMM

A further element is an owner who spoils the pet. Doting on some dogs when home creates a dog that may overmiss people when left alone. Therefore, isolation will cause tension. Dogs are great tension relievers. They act out their frustrations, sometimes digging furiously. They rarely suffer psychosomatic diseases as people do. If your pet is in the spoiled category, some steps to unspoil him will be necessary. This is probably the most difficult portion of the program to put into effect.

Who's Boss?

Ask yourself what your dog does for you. Will he come when called, sit, stay, and so on? Make a mental list. Then make a list of the things you do for your dog. Do you get his food, water, provide his shelter, open and close doors, groom him? When he wants to be petted, do you comply?

If you find yourself at the beck and call of your dog in everyday life, is it any wonder the dog may perceive you as his servant and itself as master of the relationship? Then, when you ask him to accept being isolated from you or other living things, the "master" will find it difficult or impossible to not get extremely upset and try to do something about it. The picture had best be changed for the good of the dog and owner.

Because our dogs are domesticated they never get the opportunity to mature as wild dogs do. They are forever dependent on us for food, water, access to the outdoors, and the like. It is not surprising that they become bossy. The problem digger must be changed from a bossy leader into a contented follower, at least to the point where he will stop digging.

Corrective Program

Changing a bossy dog into one that accepts your wishes is easier to describe than to put into practice. The formula is simple: Each time your dog asks you to do something for him, you merely turn the tables and ask him to do something for you. Even if the request is only to sit to gain approval, petting, or dinner, you will thus be meeting two needs of the pet. A good follower needs to function for his leader. Your pet also needs your approval, which you express with praise and petting. So whenever you are approached for some attention, you must ask the dog to sit or do something else. Then go ahead and praise and pet him, but only briefly. Avoid prolonged petting and fondling. Fondling spoils the program and the dog. This aspect of your program is the single most important one. It requires great self-control. Most of us have been well trained by our dogs to pet them whenever they want. We even do it without being conscious of it at times. However, it must be stopped to solve the problem.

When all of the previous steps are taken you will find a "new" dog in the house within a few days—a dog anxious to please, and more relaxed. Also you will be on your way to gaining a dog that begins to accept being left alone for longer and longer periods without digging.

If you have tied up your dog to keep him from digging, you should untether him. Too many animals have choked to death attempting to escape from tethers. Secure the yard if your pet is digging to escape.

Aids to Correction

A structural device that sometimes helps if the dog is digging out at a certain spot is a piece of plywood or sheet metal driven vertically two feet into the ground. Allow at least four inches of the material above ground so the dog cannot dig into it and injure itself. The only shortcoming to this barrier is that some dogs may switch their digging to a different spot. However, if it is integrated with the entire program, this seldom occurs.

Dogs that dig in gardens or yards often are repelled by substances available commercially. If you have not tried any of these, they often help if used along with this program. Listerine mouthwash is distasteful to dogs, and can be sprayed on objects.

If you have been in the habit of taking the dog out for neighborhood walks, it is a good idea to curtail this during the program. When the problem is solved and six weeks have passed you can try a walk. If it produces backsliding, walks had best be abandoned.

Follow every step of the program that applies to your situation. Be patient and optimistic. Your pet will sense your mood and improve often more quickly than you imagine possible. The result should be a more responsive, better adjusted dog.

C H A P T E R   2 1

Escaping

If your dog is trying to escape from the yard, the house, or even the car, the odds are strong that he has succeeded at least once in his efforts. One success usually stimulates more attempts in the future.

Two basic causes create escape behavior problems: the animal wants to get to somewhere, or he may be trying to get away from something. It would be too simple to say that every escapist is trying to get somewhere, since I have known dogs that were escaping to avoid ultrasonic burglar alarms or just the boredom of prolonged isolation.

One case I recall vividly involved a large German Shepherd that kept breaking out through a window, even though he had a dog door he could have used. After several window replacements and numerous veterinary visits for stitches, I was consulted. I hid behind a fence and was amazed to see a huge tomcat jump into the yard when the owners left the house for work. He stalked toward the Shepherd's dog door, stood poised outside for a few seconds, and then plunged through with a ferocious yowl.

The next instant I heard an unmistakable canine scream of terror. The crash of plate glass announced the Shepherd, airborne and on his way to a back corner of the yard where he huddled in some bushes.

It turned out that overfeeding was the cause of this problem. Quite by accident the tomcat learned that the Shepherd never finished his morning meal.

The cat was engrossed in finishing the feast when I entered the kitchen. I let out a war whoop and chased the offending tom out the dog door. At last report the cat had not been seen in the neighborhood since!

Finding the Cause

The causes for escape may be simple, goal-directed behavior aimed at freedom to roam, to get to a female dog in season or, as in our Shepherd's case, some bizarre circumstance.

To determine the cause you must investigate all the details of your dog's escape behavior. Think back to the first time it occurred.

What were the elements?

Where did the pet go?

How long did he stay wherever he went?

What did you do when you got him back? (If you punished him back at the house, you did exactly the wrong thing! Even if you punished him on his way out of the area, that probably did not help and may have reinforced the escaping.)

Correction Program

Our program for correcting escape behavior has three phases:

1. Find the cause.
2. Remove the cause as far as is practical.
3. Reshape the environment and the dog's behavior to clear up the problem.

If the cause for escaping is some attractive goal, such as freedom to roam the neighborhood or to visit the corner store for some treats from the children, very little can be done to remove the attraction. However, if the neighbors allow their own pets to run free, the direct approach to these owners is certainly justified and necessary. Escaping the yard, either by digging or jumping, is extremely difficult to clear up if irresponsible pet owners allow their animals to run free.

Whether or not neighbor cooperation is received, some structural changes can be made for diggers and jumpers. For diggers, plywood or sheet metal can be driven vertically into the ground to a depth of about two feet, leaving at least four inches of the piece of material above ground to prevent the dog's digging at it, which might result in injury.

For the jumper, a sturdy ledge can be built near the top of the fence or wall, parallel to the ground and about ten inches wide. This structure makes it impossible for the dog to gain the leverage required to boost itself over the top. If your jumper clears the entire fence or wall in one bound, a small subfence about eighteen inches high can be placed about thirty to forty-eight inches inside the wall. This will break the dog's stride and make jumping impossible.

One of my clients took another simple approach by digging a sunken garden around the wall's inside perimeter. His jumping Irish Setter made one gallant attempt at escaping, but was totally unnerved when his final stride dropped eight inches below the level of his approach run.

Even if these measures are taken, they do not by themselves cure escape behavior. We must reshape the environment even more and pay attention to possible causes before total rehabilitation can be achieved.

Use of Dog Doors

Dog doors are one of the most helpful aids in escape behavior, particularly for the dog that tries to break into or out of the house. They are also useful for a dog that digs or jumps out of the yard, especially if his goal is merely to go to the front porch and await your homecoming. The dog door relieves tension created by the monotony of periods of isolation. **The freedom to go in and out of the house at will has cleared up thousands of cases of escape behavior, with no other measures being required.** Some hard-core yard escapists have become content with the freedom to go into the house and lie down in a favorite spot rather than striving for freedom outside.

If your escaping pet cannot be trusted alone in the house, ask yourself why. If he chews up furniture or other valuables, soils inside, or engages in other undesirable behavior, consult the program in this book dealing with that particular indoor problem. Follow those instructions to the letter, and when combined with this program, you should expect success within one to six weeks.

Many rehabilitated escape artists I have known merely needed to be inside their owner's home with reassuring sights, sounds, and scents to solve the dilemma.

Easy In & Out

Getting the Dog Involved

One final step in the program addresses itself to your dog's contentment. If you do not give the dog some sort of functional activity, he will invent one, such as escaping the yard or house to patrol his property or neighborhood. Therefore, to fulfill this need you will have to ask your pet at least once a day to do something simple like sit and stay for you. Do not spend more than about three minutes on this. However, this simple functional activity can do more than anything else to relax your dog. You will be demonstrating your leadership. Dogs with leaders are more relaxed and at ease mentally.

Leaders also can play with their dogs as well as demonstrate leadership through the simple sit-stay exercise. Get a ball, a toy bone, or some article you can toss. Throw it or run with it (avoid tug-of-war if the dog has a chewing problem) to get the dog involved chasing the ball or toy. Spend no more than five to fifteen minutes in play and you will be satisfying another basic canine need—the need for exercise and the feeling of joyful abandon that comes only through play. This releases tensions in the animal and increases his contentment as discussed earlier.

Do not take the dog on walks in the neighborhood because that will extend his sense of territoriality. The play times will give him all the exercise he needs.

If you follow the program faithfully you should expect success within days or by six weeks, depending on your pet's personality, your own attention to detail, and the severity of the situation. If you have difficulty, reread the program and investigate whether you might be inadvertently missing some of the elements involved. Thousands of others have succeeded by applying the program diligently. When you have adapted him to your circumstances, you should have a reformed escape dog, and a lifelong companion that is a joy to own.

CHAPTER 22

Fearfulness (Phobias)

A puppy or adult dog gripped by fear can be pitiful, even frightening, to behold. Fear causes dogs to respond in any of three ways—toward the threat, away from it, or to freeze (play possum). This program concerns dogs that are fearful of such things as noises, sights, even certain rooms, etc. Sometimes the things that dog owners think are frightening their pets are not always the real causes for the problem but are only signals for some other event that might occur afterward. An example will illustrate this; you may find that it applies in your dog's case.

A Case History

The Fourth of July often causes serious phobias. Here is a typical case. A delightful female German Shepherd and her "family": mother, father, and three teenage girls. Gypsy was a happy-go-lucky dog and didn't seem to have a care in the world. To illustrate one of the steps for rehabilitation, we made a setup to re-create the phobia: One of the girls went out of the dog's sight and shot off a cap gun. Gypsy stopped in her tracks, began trembling violently, eyes glazed, salivating streams of fluid. The family all gathered around her, speaking sympathetically to console her. Ironically, Gypsy was locked into herself and didn't even seem aware of their presence.

Then, we all walked to the rear of our office building, leaving Gypsy alone. Everyone started to laugh and act happy, as if we were having a great time. This Jolly Time act had only been underway for two minutes when Gypsy came racing around the corner, wagging her tail as if she hadn't seen the family for a week! She had just recovered from what is often called a psychomotor seizure, i.e., no apparent physical cause.

Fact-Finding

To help in this type of case, whether your dog shows reactions as gross as Gypsy's, or is only mildly fearful, you will need to recall the very first situation in which the fearfulness occurred. In this case,

"I'm the lady who called about the tranquilizers."

the girls were having a Fourth of July party when one of the guests lit a large firecracker. It exploded close to Gypsy, whereupon she tried frantically to get out of the room. When the girls saw this, they cuddled her to try to calm her. However, one of the sisters also screamed angrily at the offending guest and shoved the boy out the front door. The dog was then taken to a bedroom and literally cuddled in bed all night. Gypsy had never been frightened of loud noises before, but from that time forward she was terrified even by car backfires.

Interpretation—Your Role

Gypsy reacted normally to the initial shock of the exploding firecracker for her type of nervous system—excitable and passive. However, the girls unwittingly provided the phobic interpretation by showing extreme reactions themselves. They literally showed the dog how to feel and react—emotionally upset, fearful. In this case, Gypsy responded inwardly (inhibitable) by freezing. Other types of dogs (excitable) may run about, wild-eyed, responding outwardly.

Analyze Your Case

The first step toward correction is to analyze your situation. Discuss the first time it occurred, how the pet reacted, and, more importantly, how you and others behaved. If you were part of the fearful interpretation, your behavior is also going to be vital in correcting the dog's problem: You will have to provide a new interpretation for the dog.

If the dog was alone when he acquired the phobia, you will need to be especially patient with him. This often happens when the owners work and some noise, storm, or other event upsets the dog. In these cases, just being left alone often produces the fearfulness, especially in puppies under six months of age.

Corrective Program

Whether or not you know all the details of the first incident, the following program still applies and should be carried out for six weeks. Don't omit any of the steps.

Learn-to-Earn Leadership

Every dog needs leadership if he is to feel secure and, hence, behave differently to formerly frightening events. To achieve this, you will have to demonstrate that you are a competent leader. Put the learn-to-earn exercise into effect: Whenever your dog seeks attention and affection, ask him, "(Name), sit," before briefly petting and praising him as a reward. Dogs cherish approval and petting. By asking them to do something, even as simple as sit, to function for approval, they soon become highly responsive to your leadership. Have him stay sitting for up to two minutes by extending the time during that first week. Also, use the learn-to-earn praise and petting exercise at mealtimes, before opening doors, putting on the leash, and whenever you get the urge to pet the dog.

Avoid fondling. Make your petting brief and upbeat. Long periods of fondling can spoil the dog and ruin any correction program. On the other hand, don't command the dog like a drill instructor. Speak naturally and avoid appearing threatening. In other words, do not be either a softy or a tyrant. After two to four days of this leadership treatment, you will begin to see the dog more eager to please. You can then start the next step in the program.

The Jolly Routine

Make arrangements so you can create the noises or situations that cause the dog's fearful behavior. Also, be prepared to produce a situation that makes your dog wag his tail and act happy. Each dog has his favorite toy or some key word that causes him to act happy. If yours does not have one, you will need to create one. Try bouncing a ball, playing with a toy, laughing—anything that causes a wagging, happy response; even rattling car keys can work.

After this groundwork is laid, produce the situation that causes the fear behavior. But, the instant you do so, produce the happy-type stimulus—the Jolly Routine—with gusto! It is marvelously effective when carried out with conviction. Don't wait for the dog to get fearful. Introduce the jolly element immediately. Not even a half-second should elapse between the fear stimulus and happy elements.

When you apply the Jolly Routine, here is what should happen: At first your dog may appear a little confused and may even fall into his fear pattern. Even so, keep up the Jolly Routine for a minute or two, then go on about some other business. Pay no further attention to the dog. After about five minutes, repeat the whole process. Do this no more than four times, twice a day if possible. Allow at least three hours between any two, complete Jolly Routine exercise setups. You will know you are succeeding when you see the dog begin to wag his tail even before you start the jolly business. Continue the process for six weeks. If you see any backsliding, merely restart the program.

Isolation Fear

If your dog becomes fearful when left alone, add the following plan to your program. Before leaving home, get all your preparations for departure completed, then sit down in the area where the fear behavior occurs. Don't pay any attention to the dog. Read a paper, drink a cup of coffee or tea, but ignore him. After five minutes, get up and leave, still ignoring the dog, and go to work or run your errands. When you return home, enter without any emotional display. Quietly say "hi" to the dog, then ignore him for at least five minutes. If there is evidence of fearful behavior that happened when you were gone, such as chewing, ignore it and clean up the mess when the dog is away from the scene and unaware of your activities.

On days off, you may do this routine two or three times, but leave three hours between each setup. If you know there are certain sounds that trigger the fearfulness, produce these on your days off. However, do not produce them and then rush back into the house. Instead, wait about five minutes before calmly entering. This demonstrates that there is nothing to be upset about and, once again, provides a leadership example.

Haircuts

Some dogs with hair that hangs over their eyes can become shy or even fearful. As mentioned earlier, if you have such a dog, do your pet a favor and tie his hair up or, better yet, cut it off. Life down on the floor is tough enough without having to look at the world through a picket fence of hair. Contrary to popular myth, "hairy-eyed" dogs don't go blind when their eyes are exposed to sunlight. This clip avoids visual "surprises" when people reach to pet or pick up the dog.

It is tough. . . to be isolated.

If the dog has been tranquilized, consult the veterinarian before starting the program. Follow instructions strictly. Be patient throughout the program. Remember, phobias in people can take years to correct. But dogs can begin to respond remarkably well in days.

A final caution: If the dog might harm himself or your property, take special precautions to avoid problems when you plan your corrective setups.

Fighting Other Dogs

When dogs fight, the primitive savagery horrifies any mentally healthy dog owner. Some unbalanced people actually promote dog fights, betting on the outcome. These sadists and masochists use their dogs as extensions for their own compulsions to hurt or to be hurt. Even so, normal dog owners can unwittingly promote dog fights.

Causes

"My dog can lick your dog" is an attitude lurking below the surface in many dog owners, especially children. Also when a stray dog is shooed away angrily in the family dog's presence, this can overstimulate the family dog's feelings about territorial protection and promote fighting.

Another cause for fighting is an attack by another dog. Often the victim thereafter reacts with extreme aggression to all other dogs. Two or more dogs in the same household may start fighting as they mature, especially if they are littermates or the same sex.

Serious fighting in family dogs usually has its roots in the way people react to the first early signs of threat displays between the pets. If you will recall these early scuffles, you can probably answer the following questions affirmatively:

- Were the dogs pulled apart?

- Was one or both of the dogs punished or angrily scolded?

These reactions, though quite normal, can actually heighten hostility between the pets. Such human actions do not necessarily get across the right message to the dogs.

When we interfere, the dogs think we are joining the fray! If one dog is punished, the other one may feel we are taking his side. This can make the dog "punish" the other at a later time. Even simple scolding can create this reaction.

After years of consulting with the owners of fighting dogs, my records show it was the *owners* who escalated these early threat displays into full-blown battles. On the positive side, however, the same owners corrected the problem by following a program to intervene in a different way with their pets.

It usually takes six weeks to correct the problem. But, if your dogs have punctured each other or have fought five or more times, more time may be required to gain peace and contentment.

Natural Pack Behavior

Before outlining the correction program it will help to consider dogs in their natural social situation—living with a pack of dogs rather than with people. In the wild, every dog has a function—a job. Hunting is a highly organized matter, and survival of the pack requires each animal to perform his function successfully. Injury or death of any member endangers the total pack welfare.

Peace and the pecking order are maintained through displays rather than serious fighting. These displays are rituals in which a dominant dog menaces an underling dog that then responds submissively by either lowering his head, perhaps even snarling as a seeming objection, rolling onto his side or back, urinating, or running away with his tail down. Seldom does any physical injury occur, and the ritual maintains harmony.

Many of these behaviors may also be seen in litters of domestic puppies. They do not persist, however, because the pups are soon placed in human homes.

Corrective Program

You may be wondering at this point if it is going to be necessary to change your home into one resembling a pack of dogs in order to correct warring dogs. No. I have found it far easier and more effective to "humanize" dogs than to "uncivilize" people. However, the success of the program depends on you and others around the dogs. You must establish a strong leadership position with the dogs and dominate the emotional climate of the environment. A goodly amount of self-discipline is required, but success can be achieved if the program is followed strictly.

The first step is to have faith in the dog's incredible ability to adapt—to change his feelings and behavior in response to changes in the environment.

In the early stages of the program you may want to keep your fighting dog or dogs separated from the adversary. Also, if your dogs fight when left alone, they must be kept separated. When we cannot control the stimulus for fighting, it would be inhumane to leave the dogs to their own fate.

Show Leadership

The first change required is to demonstrate to the pet that his people are good-natured, consistent, competent leaders. Dogs with this type of leadership seldom vie for dominance or fight.

To reach this leadership goal every person in the household must ask the dog(s) to do something to earn praise or petting. This should be something simple, such as sit, or some other thing the dog does well. This must be done each time the dog asks for attention or when people want to give him attention.

Do not order your dog to act; just ask pleasantly, then praise him when he starts to obey and pet him when he completes the act. Make your petting quick, happy, and brief—no longer than three to five seconds.

Avoid absentminded stroking or fondling. It can create jealousies and ruin your program. After about four days of this treatment you should begin to see a more responsive pet, more willing to accept direction. When this happens you are ready to go on to the next step.

The Jolly Routine

Every dog has something that makes him happy. It may be a bouncing ball or some other toy, hearing "Good dog" and happy-acting people, or a suggestion of a car ride. Whatever device turns on the happy switch with your pet, use it as the key part of what I call the Jolly Routine. This routine is used to switch the dogs from hostile to happy moods when they first come together.

The exposure of the dogs to each other can be through glass doors, a fence, on leashes, or in a free situation. You must choose how to do it, based on your ability to control the dogs and the mood of the setup.

The very instant the dogs become aware of each other, the Jolly Routine must be started. Bounce the ball, say "Good dogs," and get the tail-wagging response. Then take them away from each other, or leave them together if they seem peaceful. If they are left together, be diligent and ready to start the jolly business again if you see any sign of impending trouble, such as stiffness of gait, staring, or a tail raised high. If so, get jolly again!

Follow this routine twice daily if possible. Continue it until you see the dogs start to wag their tails before you can apply the Jolly Routine. At that time a valuable goal has been reached—a genuine conditioned switch in mood from hostility to jollity.

Carry on the program for at least six weeks to gain virtually permanent correction. Longer programs are required in more severe cases.

Away from Home

If you feel your home territory is part of the cause for fights, take the dogs to another place for the earlier setup. In any case, be sure to distract them with the Jolly Routine if either starts to urinate. The act of urinating seems a bit like muscle flexing in people—challenging.

If your dog fights other dogs in the neighborhood, do not allow him to urinate outside your own backyard. Otherwise you will be allowing him to extend his territory beyond the boundaries of his own property, which invites fighting.

Always keep in mind the program's principles:

- Gain strong leadership for all family members.

- Ask the dog(s) to earn praise and petting.

- Stop all fondling of the pets.

- Use the Jolly Routine during your formal sessions and if any sign of hostility appears.

Conduct the program in circumstances that you can control, apply good-natured determination, and persevere for at least six weeks. If this is done you should achieve peace and tranquility.

Housetraining

Believe it or not, teaching a puppy or an old dog to use a special toilet place is a lot easier than you might think—if you use this method. Why? Because it is natural to your dog. Thousands of dog owners have used the program successfully. So can you, if you will follow the directions strictly.

Be a Teacher

Keep two points in mind: First, dogs are able to learn from five weeks through old age. Before they can learn, however, they have to realize that you are going to teach them!

Second, all dogs raised in normal litters are hygienic. In early life they seek a spot to eliminate that is remote from where they eat and sleep. We people are the culprits who force them to violate this hygiene. We place doors and other barriers between them and a proper toilet area.

During this program you will use two types of rewards: verbal praise and petting. Tidbits are out. We want the pet to learn for you, not food.

To make you the teacher we will use your pet's need for praise and petting because this is natural. How many times a day does your dog ask to be petted? I'll bet it is more often than you realize. I will also bet that you respond to his requests by petting, which is only natural. Now, however, we will use these "magic moments" to teach the dog that you are a teacher as well as a petter. Here's how:

- Each time your puppy or dog asks for petting, respond by holding your hand, palm up, about a foot above his nose and saying, "Rover, sit." (Use your dog's name, of course.) Move your hand back over his ears as you speak. This makes the dog look up, which is the first step of sitting for our canine friends.

- Keep repeating "Good, sit" until the dog sits.

Then pet him on the throat and chest with your other hand for a few seconds as you repeat the praise.

If not achieved the first time, repeat the process until success is reached. When the dog sits for about five to ten seconds, release him from the command by saying "Free," then pet and praise again. Gradually increase the time during the sit until you have reached one or two minutes before you say "Free." Be sure everyone who lives with the pet follows this procedure during and even after your program. Consistent treatment from the whole family makes a better adjusted, happier pet.

Diet and Feeding

Feed at least twice a day. All dogs do not have the same digestive rates. You may have to feed a puppy up to five times daily to avoid overloading his system and causing loose, uncontrollable bowel movements. When you find the right schedule, the dog will eat and then, within a few minutes, have a bowel movement. This works out perfectly because someone must be there to feed the dog anyway, so supervision to his toilet spot is not inconvenient.

How much should you feed? Only enough to produce a formed, firm stool that you can pick up with tissue without leaving any residue. If the stool is too loose, cut down by 10 percent increments until a firm stool is achieved. If too dry, increase by 10 percent steps until the proper stool is obtained. If you see mucus or blood, or if the stools do not firm up, consult your veterinarian at once.

Do not switch diets without the veterinarian's advice. Extensive testing has proved that dogs fed varying diets are more nervous, suffer more illness, and die younger. Do not shortchange your pet's opportunity for a full life.

Feed inside the house. Remember, dogs loathe to eliminate where they eat. If your dog is urinating or defecating in a certain indoor area, try feeding him right at that spot (after cleaning it up, of course). Leave the food dish at the spot between meals for four days as a reminder against soiling that area again. Some older dogs that urinate in the house may require this food dish treatment for up to six weeks to break the habit, but it works wonders when applied with the entire program.

When and Where to Go

Immediately after your dog finishes his meal, "scoot" him good-naturedly out, ahead of you if possible, to his toilet area. Then stand still and let him sniff around for his preferred spot. The act of sniffing seems vital as a warm-up to elimination. Do not interfere by urging your pet to perform.

When the duty is performed, crouch down and point at the urine or fecal matter and say, "Good dog." Look right at the stuff, not at the dog. If the dog sniffs it, praise and pet him enthusiastically before taking him back inside.

The foregoing routine should be followed after each meal for dogs of all ages, plus on the following occasions for puppies and older dogs that are new to indoor living:

- After waking up, even from a nap

- After extreme excitement

- After drinking water

- After prolonged chewing on a toy, etc.

- If he starts to sniff as if looking for a spot to eliminate.

In about four days the pup or dog should automatically head for his proper place after meals or whenever the urge strikes. If it takes longer, be patient. When this becomes routine, phase one of the program is accomplished: the pet knows where to go.

When and Where Not to Go

During phase two of the program it is vital to keep feeding times as consistent as possible. Do not feed at 7:30 a.m. weekdays and then delay it on weekends for the sake of extra sleep. You will ruin the biorhythm of the program; your pet will become anxious and break his routine.

Dogs can control their urination up to thirteen hours, depending on activity, temperature, and other factors. For housetraining, just as with children, they must learn to "clamp down" to control their eliminations. Once learned, self-control is automatic. To help them, phase two requires that you do not let them out to the toilet area at times when you are not normally home to do so. You will accomplish little by teaching your pet to control himself Monday through Friday, but letting him out all day on Saturday and Sunday!

Whenever you see that the pet wants to "go" during the taboo hours, distract him by tossing a ball, playing with a toy, or any activity that will take his mind off the urge. This technique can succeed in three or four days with puppies. An older dog may take a bit longer. Apply the program consistently and you will win. Clients with dogs over ten years old have succeeded. So can you.

Night Supervision

If it is possible, have your pet sleep in a room with people. This promotes fewer night accidents. Dogs are inclined to become attuned to the sleeping times of their people. If given a little blanket as a bed, most dogs will sleep through the entire night.

If your dog is sneaky about urinating in the house, it may be advisable to take up his water between meals and at night. However, consult with your veterinarian first. If accidents occur only at night, try hanging a small bell on the pet's collar. This will wake you in the night. Then send the dog back to bed.

The dog's second best friend is a doggy door. If it is practical in your situation, get one. It can speed up the program significantly.

Poop 'n scoop!

Secret Cleanup

Old-fashioned house training methods tell us to grab a pup or dog, stick his nose in or near a mess, and scold or punish him physically. This kind of treatment is not necessary and may even slow down your house training program.

Instead, if an accident is discovered, just whisk your pet out to his proper toilet area. Leave him there while you clean up the mess. Make sure the dog cannot see you cleaning up the urine or fecal matter. Strangely, many animals find it rewarding to witness their people picking up their stools or urine. They often leave another "present" at the next opportunity, like a little game of "poop 'n scoop." They poop and their people scoop.

Indoor accidents can be cleaned effectively with a 50/50 solution of tepid water and white vinegar. This neutralizes the residual odor. On carpets, sponge out the area by stomping paper towels underfoot until dry.

Now that you have read this program once, read it again. Keep it handy for reference. Make sure all those living with the pet follow the program closely. If the steps are taken properly, you should expect a fastidious puppy or adult dog in four days to six weeks, depending on your situation.

Jumping on People

The jumping dog, adult or puppy, is a social menace and a very real threat, especially to pregnant women, elderly folks, and small children. If you have tried all of the generally advised corrections, such as kneeing the dog in the chest, pushing him away, scolding, or maybe even stepping on his rear toes, all to no avail, this program should be welcome because it avoids physical punishment. However, to use it successfully you first have to understand why dogs jump.

Understanding the Reasons

Friendly Jumping

Jumping up on people or other animals takes several forms. The one we see most is what I call friendly jumping. It is usually aimed at getting up to a person's face, because this is the area that communicates verbally with the dog and also emits the essence of life itself, the breath. Dogs and many other mammals put great importance on scenting the breath of those they meet. They can identify countless different people by their breath, as well as by the body odors which we constantly shed into the air. Many of these airborne chemical communicators are called pheromones. Humans long ago lost the ability to sense them.

Other friendly dogs may have had their jumping problem unwittingly encouraged by humans. Some people love to rough and tumble with their dogs, especially puppies. But some dogs do not seem able to contain this horseplay to formalized sessions, and generalize it to jumping up on all people all the time, especially when they first meet or greet them.

The dog that cannot discriminate between when and when not to jump up needs special treatment and consideration, particularly from the people who have been playing roughly with him. The dog that does not discriminate playtime from other times can become frustrated by the seeming inconsistency of people. This frustration can be expressed by even more jumping.

The answer in this situation is self-evident: The roughhousing must be stopped. When this is done, along with the other steps I will mention later, the problem can be solved.

Serious Jumping

Another kind of jumping can be called serious jumping. In the language of the wild kingdom, dogs jump to place their forepaws on pack members to express or vie for social dominance. Our domestic pups often start this behavior with their human companions.

This type of jumping can be recognized when the dog jumps and then remains still with his forepaws on the person. The proposed underling is then supposed to remain still as well, thereby signaling submission. Since few respond this way, the dog can become upset and may jump with even more determination.

Most dogs of this type are bossy in other ways as well. To solve the problem effectively, everyone living with the dog will need to follow this program strictly. Follow these directions for sexual mounting as well.

Corrective Program

Our approach to correction is straightforward and simple. **First you must spend more time with your pet,** if possible. Do not throw him out of the house to avoid the jumping.

Most problem jumping takes place when a dog first meets people. To help the pet contain his enthusiasm, you will have to **teach him some substitute behavior that is more rewarding or less frustrating than the jumping.** So, when you and others see the dog approaching, ask him to sit as you move your hand, palm upward, over his head. This will cause him to look up, and looking up is the first part of sitting for dogs.

Tell the pet "Good, sit" when he first looks upward. Be patient and repeat this process if the sitting is not achieved immediately. When the sit does happen, crouch down and pet the dog on the throat and upper chest. Avoid petting so enthusiastically that you reexcite the dog into getting up from his sit. Your crouching gives the dog a chance to get a whiff of your breath and satisfies that urge.

Involve Others

After a few days and experience with several people the dog will not require the crouch and will substitute the sit for jumping up.

Whenever you and others first greet the dog, avoid overexciting him. Stand with your side toward him rather than facing him. For some dogs the act of facing them stimulates jumping. One of the causes for this is people facing the dog defensively often raise their hands to their shoulders and say "Down." Even though the voice says down, the hands are saying "C'mon up!" Some dogs actually learn to jump up to the word "down" through this unwitting training.

You cannot control others and their movements, so you will have to teach your dog to sit when this defensive hand-raising occurs. Do this after you have achieved sit to your spoken command. Then, ask for the sit as you raise your hands to your shoulders or chest. Expect a jump or two at first, but be consistent by countering the jump with a sidestep while you repeat the command "Sit." Repeat this routine until your pet sits for the hand-raising without any need for a command. Then you will be ready to enlist the assistance of some sympathetic friends to follow the same procedure you have used.

After a few people have done it, you will have a pet who sits rather than jumps when he meets people. Also, you will have avoided all of the bad side effects of scolding and punishment.

Jumping on People Who are Sitting

If the dog jumps up when you or others sit down on a chair or sofa, the following technique works wonders when practiced for a few days on a regular basis. Each time you see the dog approaching with the intention of jumping up, before he is even close enough to you to jump, abruptly stand up and use the hand-over-his-head technique to teach him to sit. When the sit is achieved, pet the dog and then start to sit on the chair again. This is a critical moment in the plan because your movement to sit may trigger your dog to get up. If you see this start to happen, straighten up again. The dog should settle, whereupon you must start again to sit.

This little routine can be extremely subtle. Sometimes just the act of starting to bend your knees to sit can cause the dog to start to get up or jump. So watch carefully and react instantly.

If you use body language consistently with dogs you will communicate effectively. And the better your communication, the better the control of your dog will be. Thus, from teaching your dog not to jump up, you will also gain an improved relationship with him.

Try these techniques with dogs other than your own that jump up. As you become more expert with the technique, you will find yourself less troubled by all jumping dogs.

Follow the program with patience and sincere dedication and you should see success within a few days or weeks, depending on how often you put it to work. The rewards in terms of a well-mannered pet will far outweigh the effort invested.

Killing Animals

If your dog has killed other animals, you are faced with one of the most difficult problems. Basically, three types of animal killers are found, and the types are defined according to the dog's emotional state during the attack. They are:

- Angry killers

- Playful killers

- Predatory, cold-blooded killers.

If your dog kills in anger, a complete program can be found for him in the chapter on Fighting Other Dogs, and that program should be instituted immediately and followed faithfully.

Playful versus Predatory Killers

Playful types usually target on birds, gophers, fowl, and other small mammals. This program will deal with that problem.

Predatory, cold-blooded types are the most difficult to rehabilitate and require extreme dedication to succeed. Most predatory types do not eat their prey; it is only their approach to killing that is predatory. Deliberate stalking, lying in wait, attacking the target animal at the base of the neck (a predator kill area) are the hallmarks of these dogs. Their entire procedure can be bone-chilling to witness, since their prey are usually totally unaware of their intentions until too late.

Most animal killers in my case files have a history of too little activity with their owners. This is often coupled with a history of the owners sicking their pet on stray animals that entered his territory. Even the innocent act of shooing animals away from the property can be interpreted by some dogs as a license to attack and kill. If this has been your unwitting error, you will now need to reverse your course and appear happy when intruders appear.

Corrective Program

Most animal-killing dogs are leader types. That is, they tend to be bossy in their relationships with their family members. Some are loners. In either case, the dog must learn that you and others in the household are going to teach him. This is more difficult with loners, since they do not show as much need for attention. However, this program has succeeded nicely, even with some highly independent types.

The first step is to gain a strong orientation toward yourself in order to establish your leadership role with the dog. It requires that you ignore your pet completely except to feed him, supervise his toilet activities, and whatever other activities are absolute necessities, such as opening doors. You must cut off all play and petting, and even avoid eye contact until the point is reached where the dog appears frustrated and in dire need for attention or approval. With some independent types, this ignore-the-dog routine may require up to four days before the desired orientation is gained. At this point you can proceed to the second step.

Step two requires that you now show your pet affection, but only after he has responded to some direction from you. This direction can be as simple as asking him to sit or lie down. Then you should pet him briskly with upbeat praise for no longer than about five seconds.

Avoid all soft, prolonged petting or fondling. If your dog does not perform a sit for you, teach him.

Teaching sit requires first that you teach come. This is important in this program. The stay will also be needed when exposing the dog to target animals later. Teach the come, sit, stay exercise (see chapter 7) involving all family members, for at least a week before proceeding with the following part of the program.

Introducing "Prey" Animals

When you feel confident that your dog is oriented to you as leader, test him. Obtain the cooperation of the owner of another dog or cat (if they are your pet's prey) or get a chicken, hamster, or other such animal and show your dog how to feel and behave around him. This is where the real essence of your relationship with your dog will become clear. You must be the dog's emotional leader, and you must act happy about the appearance of the other animal. However, before you undertake the introduction, make sure your setup is secure for all concerned.

Here are some ways to make the initial exposures to prey animals. These provide safety in the event the dog overrides your control:

- Have your dog on leash if suitable barriers are not available.

- Have the prey animal on leash or in an enclosure that cannot be broken through.

- With small breeds, have a sliding glass door between the animals. This may not suffice with larger dogs, if they charge the glass.

- Hold the target animal yourself.

Whatever your situation dictates, plan the setups so that you can be in control.

The Jolly Routine

When your dog first notices the other animal, you must act happy about it. Get a ball or some other toy that your dog enjoys and bounce or toss it. Dominate the emotion of the occasion. Get your dog involved with you, rather than the other animal. The moment your dog pays attention to you, praise him and pet him briskly. When this is achieved, take away the other animal. Allow three hours to pass before beginning another Jolly Routine.

Follow this plan until the mere appearance of the prey animal turns your pet's attention to you, rather than toward it. At this point you can start bringing the two closer together. You may also benefit from standing alongside the other animal, facing your dog. This side-by-side approach causes your dog to see you with the other animal, showing friendliness. When your dog appears to accept the former prey, you should stop the session happily and remove the target animal or your dog, whichever situation fits your setup.

Be sure not to hold your dog on a tight leash as you approach the other animal. This is a classic method of training attack dogs. Many animal killers will appear happy and delighted to be teased in this way. But, when given the freedom to get to the prey, they attack with heightened ferocity.

Corrective Habits to Form

If you are in the habit of walking your dog in the neighborhood, this must be stopped, as well as allowing any urination off your own property. Most animal killers have extended their rightful home boundaries by wetting their "brands" outside their own area.

If your dog "worries" a fence line by pacing, running, or barking, keep him inside as much as possible and supervise his time in the yard with play. Practice come, sit, stay in the yard to get his mind off the barrier.

This program will require a minimum of three and a maximum of six weeks' practice to succeed. Even then, periodic refresher sessions are helpful for permanent rehabilitation.

Leash Straining

Who is walking whom? This question pops into my mind whenever I see owners being dragged down the street by their dogs. Most of my cases involve dogs that have learned to live with the discomfort of a choke chain, pinch collar, or even a leather collar. Some of them stop pulling only long enough to cough or even regurgitate, take a few breaths, then continue struggling forward. Most people have no idea that their frustrated leash puller might actually suffer physical injury during the daily tug-of-war. However, in a Swedish study by the noted behaviorist Anders Hallgren of four hundred dogs that were x-rayed, sixty-three percent were found to have spinal injuries. Of the injured dogs with neck injuries, ninety-one percent had experienced harsh jerks on the leash or were serious leash strainers. Among aggressive or overactive dogs, seventy-eight percent had spinal injuries.

Corrective Program

Most leash-strainers pull on a taut leash in response to the leash getting taut. It follows that if you never let the leash pull on the dog, he can't pull back. Of course, this is easier said than done.

This prompted me to develop and patent the Sof-Touch™ Safety Training Leash and to stop recommending the popular leash "pop" or "jerk–release" methods.

For at least four days before working on the actual problem, the owner should use the door "Freedom Dasher" technique mentioned earlier, but couple it with the following exercises. All family members old enough to do it effectively should participate. The dog should be wearing a regular flat buckle collar. Our "learn to earn praise and petting" routine should also be used every day

First, around the house and then the year, all family members should watch carefully for any time the dog starts to rush ahead. At that instant, give a single handclap or hand slap on the thigh and reverse direction abruptly while saying "Good dog." The dog should follow, at which time more praise and petting is awarded. If the dog again runs ahead, the process is repeated until the dog stays alongside or starts following you, rather than leading.

When this step has been accomplished, put on the leash and repeat the exercise with the dog dragging the lead. Take care that the leash does not snag on objects or under doors.

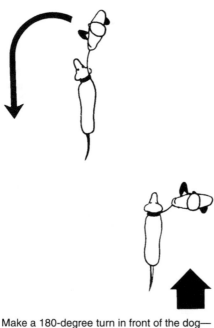

Make a 180-degree turn in front of the dog—accompanied by a handclap—when the dog begins to move ahead of you.

Make the session brief—no more than ten minutes—even if 100 percent success is not achieved. End it on a correct response and praise your dog profusely.

When the dog either follows or stays beside you, proceed to an enclosed area like a neighbor's fenced back yard or an empty tennis court for the next steps. First, the dog must learn the Sof-Touch™ feel. Start in an area with no strong distractions. Attach the leash to the collar, grasp it about halfway between the snap and the handle with your left hand. Hold your hand firmly against your waist. Leave the leash slightly slack. Hold the excess leash in your right hand. Stand still with your dog on the left side and wait until

Hold the Sof-Touch™ leash against the waist. If the dog doesn't strain, taking a few steps forward will usually stimulate him.

As the leash tightens, stop, holding fist and leash firmly to your waist. Remain still until the dog eases the pressure.

The instant the dog begins to ease the pressure, praise lavishly. You may also crouch and praise. Repeat until the dog eases up on his own.

he forges or pulls. Allow the elastic in the leash to stretch to its limit. Keep your hand firmly against your waist. Don't jerk, pull back, or ease up. The dog will eventually ease the pulling. When he starts to ease up, quickly crouch down and happily say, "Good dog!" Keep your left side toward the dog. Continue praising as long as the ease-up lasts. When the dog either comes to you or eases up all the way, praise him lavishly, then stand up and repeat the process. When the dog settles down, remains oriented to you, and the leash remains slack, praise with gusto—you've reached your primary objective. Don't train more than fifteen minutes. If there's time left, go to a new area with more distraction and repeat the process. Always end lessons on a successful note with lots of happy praise.

Leave at least two-and-one-half hours between sessions, and hold the next session in a different area. After several days with no straining, you can take off the elastic and have a regular six-foot nylon leash. Reapply the elastic and reinforce the training as needed.

Balky Dogs or Puppies

Most balky dogs are either young or have had some bad experiences with leashes. However, the method for building their confidence is the same. It may test your patience, but the results are worth it.

From a position with the dog on your left side, with both of you facing the same direction, suddenly step forward about four paces. Do not hold the leash, but just let the dog drag it. If the dog starts to move with you, praise him, pat your left thigh, and keep moving, taking shorter, quicker steps, which will help hurry the dog. If the dog catches up, stop, crouch with your left side toward him, and praise and pet lavishly.

Getting Him Moving

If the dog balks totally, simply crouch, clap, and praise happily. This should bring him to your side for more praise and another try at starting out. Keep repeating this for three successful approaches, then take the leash at full length and do it again. **Don't let the leash pull.** After a few successes, the dog should start moving with you, and you are on your way for longer walks. In the early stages of this routine, balky dogs may require that you actually run away from them to get them moving.

If your dog starts to grow roots and doesn't move for any of these inducements, try the run-away, crouch, and clap routine. Then stand up and run a half circle with your left side toward him and crouch, clap, and praise from a position directly behind the dog. If the dog starts to turn with you while you're running the half circle, praise him and pat your left thigh. Be sure that during your circling you do not approach the dog or you'll be communicating the wrong idea. If anything, gradually work away from him.

Puppies seem to have a critical field of vision in this balky dog problem. Unless you get far enough away, where they cannot see you clearly, they seem content to sit there. The critical distance can be up to thirty feet with pups less than three months old, and farther in some cases.

If your dog is such a problem that none of this works, it is best to get professional help from someone who believes in nonyanking methods of leash training before tackling the problem in a class situation where distractions can overwhelm the pet. Be sure to secure the services of someone who will teach you to solve the problem, rather than try to do it for you.

Old Age Problems

When does old age begin in a dog? It varies, by breed. Here are the most obvious signs:

- Graying of the coat

- Cataracts

- Loosening of teeth

- Physical stiffness

- Increased sleeping and less activity.

With these as signposts, a student of dogs can quickly recognize that some breeds age more quickly than others, especially the larger breeds, such as Saint Bernards and Great Danes. Little dogs not only live longer, but also show signs of old age later. So, size and health care probably influence longevity more than any other factors. Let's examine some of the problems that can accompany aging in dogs.

Blindness

As with people, many dogs gradually lose their sight as they age. However, the dog has another sense that can take the place of a cane to sense things he might bump into when making his way about the house or yard—his keen sense of smell. In fact, you may have noticed that blind dogs usually keep their noses to the floor or ground as they walk about. This allows them to smell the familiar pathways and avoid objects.

I have found another scent aid that makes life a little easier for blind dogs. This was successful with our Dalmatian that went blind at six years of age, but led a fairly active life for another four and a half years.

Here is the system: apply a scented polish to all upright obstacles in the house and outdoors. This includes chair legs, door jambs, TV sets, and so forth. The dog will quickly identify this scent with things that are "up and down" and avoid them. For horizontal dangers, such as steps, wires, and low walls, apply a different scent. I used to spray such things with a mildly scented hair spray about once a week. It did the trick nicely and saved a lot of nose scrapes.

Voice Contact

As dogs go blind they may appear to become easily startled, especially when touched unexpectedly. I have seen this lead to biting in some cases. So the rule with blind dogs is always to speak to them before touching them. If this is practiced, you will soon see the dog moving his head to "feel" for the hand that is going to touch him. This is especially true with strangers. When introducing your blind dog to strangers, have them sit in a familiar place and speak to the dog. Have them hold their hand below the level of the dog's chin, palm up, so the dog can find him by scent and nuzzle it.

Some blind dogs seem bothered by having the tops of their heads or backs petted; confine the petting to under the chin, on the throat and chest. This keeps the blind dog's head up and seems to relieve any worries he might have.

Blind dogs may also need "company" when going out to their toilet places. If this is a problem, it is best to put the animal on a twice-a-day feeding schedule and develop a twice-a-day rhythm for bowel movements. Be sure not to overfeed the dog. Feed just the amount that produces a formed, firm stool. Above all, be sure to leash a blind dog in areas that could be dangerous.

Deafness

Hand Signs and Body Language

Whether old or young, deaf dogs can be taught by capitalizing on their vision. Body language and hand signals can speak like thunder to these animals. However, avoid shouting at partially or totally deaf dogs. Shouting can confuse them and they often respond by barking. And nothing is worse than a constantly barking deaf dog—everyone is bothered by it but the dog!

The deaf dog must learn to pay visual attention to you at all times when you are out with him. To teach this, get some dried beans and make several small beanbags. Then take the dog to a safe area and, each time the dog takes his eyes off you, toss a beanbag at his legs. When he responds, you must crouch down and make "come-hither" gestures with your hands. Do not lean or move toward the dog, as this tells him to back up away from you. Have at least one of these "pay attention to me" sessions daily, concluding each session when your pet keeps his attention on you for several minutes without using the beanbags.

After a few of these lessons, you should notice your pet keeping his attention on you without your having to toss a single bag. You will then have succeeded.

Proceed to places with stronger distractions until you are sure of the dog's attention at all times, under all conditions. In dangerous areas, such as next to streets, it is a good idea to keep a leash, perhaps even up to thirty feet long, on the dog. This provides maximum safety. Once you have your deaf dog's attention, teaching him to sit-on-sign is relatively simple.

Incontinence

Lack of bladder or bowel control can occur in dogs of any age. Your veterinarian can advise you about special treatments, such as low doses of female hormones for females who cannot control their urine, geriatric vitamin supplements, and special diets. Whether the problem is with urine or stools, the doctor's diet must be carefully followed.

Overfeeding in cases of bowel incontinence is a no-no. The amount fed must produce a stool that is firm. Your pet will have difficulty exercising any control over loose stools. Once the quantity and consistency of the diet are well established, elimination should begin to stabilize and become regular. When this point is reached, proper supervision is all that is needed for success.

Toilet Supervision

Toilet time and place should be as consistent as possible. If necessary, feed your pet in a spot easily accessible (but not too close) to his toilet area. This proximity often creates a habit of evacuating immediately after eating—a most desirable result, since you must be home to feed the pet, and it is little bother then to supervise the toilet activities.

Bladder incontinence can be more difficult to control. If veterinary advice allows it, water can be made available only at mealtimes and before bedtime. However, your veterinarian must approve and set the schedule. It is most helpful if the incontinent pet is taken to his toilet place at the following times:

- After waking (even from a nap)

- After eating or drinking

- Following any play or unusual excitement

- After any extensive chewing activity

- Before bedtime.

Happy, sincere praise must be given when the "duty" is concluded at the proper place. If you focus your initial praise at the very spot that has been soiled, the dog may come over and sniff it. That is good, since it helps to fix the spot in the animal's memory bank, via his keen sense of smell.

In some cases where physical control is literally impossible, the problem will persist. In these situations, inexpensive pet diapers, available from the veterinarian or pet store, can be used to contain the problem. Urine or a formed stool will not be cripplingly unpleasant for the animal.

Irritability

Many dogs grow old with full vigor and remain in excellent spirits. Others, for various reasons, become more retiring and seem to seek solitude or, at least, peace and quiet. Some old dogs object to being disturbed. Keeping in mind that old age has his own set of behavioral rules, the best advice is to follow the old rule and let sleeping dogs lie. A little crotchetiness in old age is not news to anyone over the age of reason. If there are children in the house with such a pet, they should be taught to leave the animal alone. If this is impossible, such as may be the case with non-family children, the dog should then be separated from the area to avoid any harassment.

It bears repeating, especially in cases of elderly pets, that veterinary care often must be intensified for their well-being, their behavioral acceptability, and our own peace of mind. It is an excellent practice to report to the doctor gross or even mild changes in the behavior or condition of your pet.

As in cases of incontinence, it takes just a little understanding and consideration to afford your pet the luxury of growing old with dignity and grace. In families with children, such a program instills respect for the elderly, one of civilized humankind's most laudable traits.

CONSISTENCY IS ESSENTIAL

1.

2.

Overprotectiveness

If your adult dog or pup has shown signs of overprotectiveness, consider yourself fortunate if he has not yet bitten anyone. Many dog owners who see the first signs of protectiveness in their pets later fail to recognize the danger when overprotectiveness emerges. As a matter of fact, some people feel good and even encourage the behavior until a bite occurs.

Causes of the Problem

To correct the problem let us first look at the causes. Overprotection results from a combination of the dog's built-in capabilities to protect members of his group, whether human or canine, and the actions of the group members themselves. In other words, the way you and other family members have reacted to your dog's first signs of protectiveness may have contributed to the problem.

In today's society it is quite normal to feel insecure to some degree. Radio, TV, and the newspapers pummel our senses with a great deal of violence. Then, when a stranger approaches our door and our dog shows early signs of protecting us, we may feel somehow reassured. It is uncanny the way dogs seem able to sense our emotional reactions to such situations. And these emotions often reinforce the dog's aggressiveness. In this way we can unwittingly contribute to the problem.

In other cases family members deliberately praise the behavior, even urging the pet to menace outsiders. We see this most often when children are involved.

Owner Insecurity

Another unwitting contributor to the problem is the owner who secretly feels insecure and allows the dog to take the role of leadership. In any relationship a dog has with people or other dogs, one or the other is going to be leader. When the dog is allowed to assume this role, he often tends to overdo his territorial and group protectiveness.

As you may have gathered, it takes a bit of soul-searching on the owner's part to find the role he or she may play in an overprotection problem. It also requires carefully controlled emotions and strict adherence to this program to achieve success in molding the overprotective dog into a dependable pet that will properly protect his people.

Bossy Dog

Consider seriously your relationship with your dog: What goes on in daily life with him?

- When you leave home, does the dog try to beat you out the door?

- If you go to another room and close the door, does the dog get upset?

- When you embrace someone, are there any signs of jealousy?

- Does your dog seem to demand a great deal of petting? And do you respond by giving him what he wants?

- Would you be disappointed if your pet showed some other person preference over you?

If your dog is overprotective about you, and if you answered some of these questions "yes," you may be starting to appreciate your part in the problem. Furthermore, the chances are that you are not at fault. It is normal for a dog owner to feel emotionally comforted by the pet's affection. The problem is whether the dog or the owner is directing the occasions and duration of displays of affection.

If the dog gets petted every time he desires, it is natural that he may begin to object if other people come around and interrupt this activity. If he shows his objections with overprotectiveness, and the owner either scolds or tries to reassure him, the problem usually becomes more serious.

In other words, the pet is not really protecting his people, but protecting his selfish relationship with them, that is, his "right" to have his own way with them.

If the pet is punished physically or put away when visitors arrive, he can quickly learn to hate the sight and sound of all future visitors.

So much for the various causes of the problem. The important thing now is to enter into his correction with an enlightened attitude, avoiding things that played a part in the problem's development.

Corrective Program

An overprotective dog requires a program of broad socialization with lots of different people. Furthermore, he needs you, his leader, to show him how to behave in order to build his confidence about people. The pet that does not feel confident about people cannot learn to recognize those with unfriendly intentions. Such a dog may be fine for military guarding work but is dangerous as a family pet. So take your dog out to meet people, show him how to feel and behave by acting friendly yourself with those whom you know and trust.

When you first meet people, try to stand alongside them and chat for a while. Do not face them. Face to face, in the dog's view, signals a confrontation. When you are at a person's side the pet perceives you as friendly with that person.

If you take your dog out on a leash, make sure you do not allow him to strain the leash when you meet people. Holding a dog back from other people by a leash is a technique used in training attack dogs.

If you have a dog with hair that hangs over his eyes, do your pet a favor and tie it up, or better yet, cut it off. As mentioned elsewhere, life down on the floor is tough enough without having to look at the

"You can bring Fury in now, Mrs. Caslick."

world through a picket fence. This will avoid visual surprise when people reach to pet or pick up the dog. Contrary to a popular myth, "hairy eyed" dogs do not go blind when their eyes are exposed to sunlight.

Gain Confidence

If you do not feel confident of your ability to control your dog on a leash, find a humane, competent trainer who will teach you how to handle the leash. Avoid trainers that want to take your dog by the leash and train him for you. Such treatment only makes you seem less competent with the leash by comparison with an expert.

Pet Wisely

Along with your program of socialization, general environmental adjustments are required. In most cases of overprotection, the dogs have pretty well trained their people to pet them whenever the dogs want it. The dogs stimulate and the people respond. The leaders say "Pet me," and their subjects obey!

The worst thing I could advise you to do is to stop petting your dog. But do turn around the stimulus-response pattern of the relationship. When your dog approaches to ask for some affection and petting, you now merely ask him to sit and then go ahead and pet him, making the petting brief and happy. Avoid excessive fondling, which tends to spoil the dog and will ruin your program.

After a few days of this treatment your dog will begin to realize he must function by following your lead, to gain the social gratification he needs. This is good. You may also find the dog more willing to please you in other life situations. He will tend to be less competitive going through doors, more content and relaxed.

In the early stages of this routine the very bossy dog may resist sitting for you and go away. If this happens, just ignore him. Pouting is great self-therapy, and the dog will come around in two to four days. Do not feel rejected. Just wait it out and you will gain your position of leadership.

Use Toys

A final note about your socializing program—if your dog likes to play fetch or chase a ball, use this device with people who come to visit, at the park, and in all the situations where overprotection has been evident. Give the ball to other people and let them toss it to help strengthen the dog's confidence. Act jolly and confident yourself and you will set the best example for your dog.

On the other hand, if *you* do not feel confident, avoid having the session of socialization. You will transmit your feelings to the pet and your work will be counterproductive. Wait until another day when you feel better about it.

Follow this program and at the end of six weeks you should have a dog that is confident, friendly, and still able to protect if and when the need genuinely arises.

C H A P T E R   3 0

Self-Mutilation

The dog that chews or licks himself severely enough to cause injury certainly starts doing it for some reason. At the outset, the reason is often physical, but it can become a psychological-physical problem. For this reason, a correction program requires that you follow your veterinarian's advice to the letter. A letdown on the medical treatment may trigger irritation of the area involved and remind the pet to start chewing or licking again. By the same token, it is necessary to adhere to the behavioral element or the physical condition can worsen.

Motivation

The motivation for self-mutilation in dogs is quite different from the self-destructive motivation in people. I have never heard of a dog consciously wanting to harm or destroy himself through this behavior. As a matter of fact, the opposite appears more likely. Wolves have been reported to chew off a foot in order to escape a leg-hold trap. The obvious goal is saving rather than destroying their lives.

So the chances are good that your dog is chewing or licking himself, not neurotically, but to relieve some real irritation. At least it probably started out that way.

On the other hand, many dogs start to lick or chew themselves when left alone. Boredom can cause tension, a condition dogs can relieve through licking or chewing. Other dogs just do not accept being left alone. Thence the tension and the problem.

Corrective Program

Whatever may be causing the problem, the remedy is the same: Give your pet something to do to relieve the tension. One of the most important facets of self-mutilation cases I find is that the dogs are not required on a consistent basis to earn their petting and praise.

However, after our correction plan is in effect for a few days, they begin to relax, become more responsive to their owners' directions, and appear more contented. The way to achieve this is not difficult, but it requires self-control on everyone's part. More about this later on.

Use Play

Play is important in the lives of all dogs, both domestic and wild. People often forget this under the pressures of today's busy routines. So one part of your program is to spend a few minutes a day, in the morning if possible, playing with your dog. Toss a ball or toy, or run about the room or yard and let the pet chase you. Get his tail wagging! This intense, happy interaction is the type of activity that brings your dog out of himself and more in touch with you. Avoid playing tug-of-war, which can make the dog even more orally inclined when you leave him alone.

Defuse Emotion

Another element of your program is to defuse the emotions related to your coming and leaving home. This is not easy to do, but it will teach the dog that being left alone is not all that upsetting. This helps relieve the tensions that can result in self-mutilation. So, before leaving, spend a quiet five minutes or so in the area the dog will occupy when you are gone. Do not pay attention to the dog at all. Avoid even making eye contact. Then get up and leave without so much as a word. This sets a quiet, relaxed example for the dog when you are away.

When you come home, say a friendly "Hi," and then go on about some other business for at least five minutes. When you do greet the dog, do so in an area away from the door by which you arrived. This helps relieve your pet's intense fixation on homecoming. The result is that the contrast in being with you or without you is lessened, making it easier to be alone.

After the self-mutilation has been cleared up for six weeks you may revert to warmer homecomings on arrival, but watch for backsliding. Curtail the welcomes if it happens.

Now for the most difficult part of the plan: To start your dog on his way to earning praise and petting, you must *ask him to do something*. Make it simple. Ask the dog to sit, then say "Good dog" as soon as he starts to sit, petting him when he sits down all the way. Make your petting quick, happy and brief—not more than about five seconds long.

Avoid Fondling

More than any other action, fondling makes dogs introverted, and self-mutilation is a sign of introversion. Do not deny praise or petting, just be sure it is earned.

If the dog starts to pay attention to the mutilated area, instantly distract him with some sound or activity. Make the distraction sudden, like a slap on a table top or a quick movement toward another area. Avoid using your voice, or the correction will become dependent on your presence.

Conditioned Response

After you have applied a few corrections, you should notice the dog start to look at the spot, begin to lick or chew himself, but stop before you even have a chance to apply the correction. This is the conditioned response that will tend to be effective in your absence. Together with all other elements of the program, this conditioning is vital to success.

Continue every aspect of the program until the area of mutilation has remained clear for about six weeks. Then you may be sure the problem has been corrected. If you see any backsliding, simply reinstate the entire program for a few days.

If you and all who live with the pet follow the plan with optimism, you should start to notice results in a few days and a total correction in a few weeks.

C H A P T E R   3 1

Shyness

Shy dogs or puppies stir strong emotions in people: pity, embarrassment, even anger when the dog urinates submissively. Most people want to help shy dogs because they seem unhappy or frightened, but much more is at stake in the long run. Shyness must be dealt with immediately or it can escalate into fear biting, escaping, fear of noises, etc. Fortunately, dogs usually respond quickly to this program, and most people who use it claim they feel intensely rewarded and proud of their rehabilitated pet.

Understanding the Problem

Dogs that have been shy from puppyhood were usually isolated and enjoyed very limited contact with people. The critical age for socializing puppies is between five and thirteen weeks of age. Kennel-bred puppies often miss meaningful exposure to humans. If they join a human household after three to four months of age, they often form attachments with only one person, avoiding all others. As they mature beyond six months of age in this "one-person-dog" situation, shyness can develop into outright hostility toward outsiders.

Shyness differs from fearfulness. Wolves, coyotes, and other wild members of the canine family are shy, but not because they are afraid of people; this is self-preservation at work. If wild canines are born and raised in human homes, and socialized with lots of people, they behave somewhat like regular house dogs. However, wild, mature wolves, etc., can rarely be socialized. Unlike these wild cousins, if your dog lacks early socialization, he can still be socialized, but it requires lots of carefully supervised socialization exercises.

Learned Shyness

Some normally raised dogs actually learn shyness. They may have been frightened, overhandled, unwittingly mishandled, or even abused. These dogs also need a socializing program, but they usually require exposure only to the particular things that trigger their shyness, such as groups of people, crowds, children, other dogs, etc.

Let's examine some of the important behavioral signs of shyness:

- Does he avoid all people, including you?

- Does he urinate when approached, or when approaching people? If so, consult the program for wetting submissively.

- How does he behave when you approach him? Does he snarl, freeze, or wildly try to escape? If he snarls, use the program for aggression to owners. If he freezes, he is showing a passive defense reflex. If he tries to escape, he is showing an active flight defense reflex.

Correcting the Problem

Shy dogs lack confidence and have not yet learned to trust people. This program helps you to help the dog gain confidence and trust. As you begin to see confidence develop, both of you will begin to enjoy life a great deal more. You must avoid all harshness; exercise patience and understanding. It will be worth the effort. Even dogs older than four years of age have become outgoing, happy pets after going through the program.

Dogs cannot be forced or "trained" to trust us. We earn trust through consistent, humane treatment. Because of this, you and others meeting the dog will need to avoid all signs of threat, and behave so as to invite the dog to approach. This builds trust and allows self-confidence to take root and grow. Toward these goals, let's consider how to remove signs of threat.

Don't "Front" the Dog

In the animal world, large size and standing face to face are threatening. A gruff or shrill voice can also signal a threat. If you stare, stand stock-still, smile, or open your eyes extra wide, the dog may perceive a threat, even a prelude to attack. Where you stand within a room, or in relation to other people, can also threaten a dog. For instance, shy dogs can be attracted to you if you are near a wall, but are not easily attracted if you are out in the middle of the room.

Setting Up the Exercises

Setups need to involve you (or the person of whom the dog is not shy) and/or others of whom the dog is, or may be, shy. In the following exercise, we will assume "you" are the trusted person and we'll call those of whom the dog is shy "strangers." Here are the behavioral principles for you to follow:

- Stage the exercises in a room with which the dog is familiar. Enough space is needed to allow everyone to move several steps without crowding him; fifteen square feet is about the minimum.

- Position strangers about three feet away from the wall in the area, but in the dog's view. Have strangers stand sideways to the dog, crouch, sit on the floor, or even lie face down if he is not attracted by any of the former postures. (We'll explain later about lying face down.)

- When the dog approaches, strangers must not speak or reach for him, or even look at the dog. Let him approach and investigate at his own pace. Allow up to twenty minutes for him to make his approach. Don't rush him.

- If he doesn't approach or tries to leave the area, have one stranger take a position so the dog must pass by him, but he does not block the dog's escape route. Then, have another stranger move nonchalantly so as to make the dog approach another stranger if he wants to avoid him or leave the area. Even passing close to a person of whom he is shy is a positive sign. Repeat this passing-by exercise until the dog has passed by everyone involved.

- Using the "already trusted" person (you), bridge that trust from yourself to the strangers. Sit on the floor together, side by side, so the dog must pass by the strangers to reach you. Let the dog investigate.

When the dog has made that first positive step, stop the session, ignore the dog, and have another session after about three hours. This gives the dog's learning experience time to sink in.

In the meantime, of course, avoid those possibly threatening situations. Once the ice is broken, you will find the dog becoming increasingly more confident.

Case Examples

You will need to adapt further socializing principles to your situation and dog. The best way we can illustrate such adaptation is by the following example.

A couple bought a handsome, seven-month-old male Irish Setter from a breeding mill kennel. The dog, named Hank, took to Fran, the wife, immediately, but was shy to the point of showing fear of her husband, Jim, and everyone else. To start gaining closer contact with Jim, Fran tried allowing Hank to get up on the furniture beside her. When Jim approached them, Hank would get down, run into the bedroom closet, and hide in a dark corner. Lately he had started growling at anyone who approached the closet. Fran's setups were making things worse.

Hank's condition is called *kennelosis*, which is common in dogs left in kennels beyond fourteen weeks of age. Adapting the foregoing behavioral principles for correction, Fran sat on an outdoor couch while Jim sat on a chair beside her. Hank got up on Fran's couch and lay down. Then Fran and Jim got up and walked, side by side, toward a gate that led to their car. The dog came along but stayed at Fran's heels. They then turned around, returned to the seating area, and Fran and Jim sat on two chairs, located at opposite ends of the couch, leaving the couch unoccupied. Hank appeared confused by this switch, whined a little, and then tried to climb into Fran's lap.

She stood up each time he started to get up. After about ten attempts to get on her lap, Hank jumped onto the patio couch, putting his head over as close as possible to Fran. After about five minutes, Fran and Jim repeated the walk to the gate and came back and sat on the couch. They were amazed when Hank got onto the couch next to Fran, at the end of the couch. They got up again and returned, but this time they sat on the couch and only left enough space between them for Hank. They were delighted when Hank jumped up and actually licked Jim's hand before lying down. The ice was broken and they were on their way to success.

It is important to note, during this entire procedure, neither owner paid any attention to Hank. No one said his name, made eye contact, or faced him. Hank was allowed the opportunity to make his own adjustments at his own pace to the situation. The complete exercise took one hour.

They repeated the same exercise, in principle, in the house. Jim started feeding Hank, twice a day. In less than a week, they were conducting socialization exercises which included their friends, then children.

Another example was a shy dog that loved to chase and fetch a ball. The same principles were applied, but the bridge between trusted people was the ball. It takes patience, but if the principles are applied, you can design a plan, too.

Extreme Cases

When the dog is shy of everyone, extreme measures may be required. Here are some helpful initial steps to apply. When you feed the dog, place the food dish between you and the dog. Then, sit down about five feet from the dish with your back turned toward the food and the dog.

When you are home, take up the water dish. When the dog is good and thirsty, fill the bowl and use this sit-down technique. If he will not approach food or water, lie face down about six feet from the dish. This prone approach is usually highly successful with abused dogs who have been highly traumatized.

Patience Pays

These examples illustrate the principles that allow shy dogs to develop trust and build self-confidence. If you have patience in developing your program and avoid trying to accomplish everything in a rush, you should see positive results after your very first setups with your dog. Allow up to six weeks to reach a point where your dog begins enjoying life with confidence and trust.

Swallowing Non-Foods

If your dog swallows things that have no nutritional value, he has a condition called *pica*. Pica is sometimes seen in pregnant women and people with intestinal parasites or a certain iron deficiency. These also cause pica in dogs, and your veterinarian is the only person qualified to diagnose them. If your pet is on a program of medication, follow the doctor's directions to the letter or the behavioral phase of your program will suffer.

Identifying the Cause

Certain factors seem to be common in cases of pica. You may find one or more of these in your pet's background:

- The dog has been extremely oral from puppyhood.

- He will chew on himself when deprived of other articles.

- When the problem began, people would pull things from his mouth.

- The dog enjoys playing tug-of-war.

Although these elements are found in some dogs that do not suffer from pica, they appear with consistency in those that do have problems.

Once pica becomes a habit, major problems can result. If your pet is so affected and has not required surgery to remove something he has swallowed, consider yourself lucky.

Some of the psychological forces at work in the condition need consideration in order to understand the correction methods.

Puppies, just like human offspring, seem to want to put everything new in their mouths. Pups usually decide the article is good to chew or they reject it. Swallowing it is probably the last thing in their plan at this stage. When people pull the article out of the pup's mouth before a decision can be made, some animals develop a stronger desire for it. Also, the puppy may learn that taking such things in his mouth brings attention, even if negative, and so he carries on the practice.

Feeding only once a day leaves a dog with an empty stomach for up to nineteen hours out of each twenty-four, which invites pica. So it is a requirement of this program to **feed at least twice daily**.

Symbolic Pica

A most common element in pica is the eating of articles that belong to or symbolize the owner. This usually occurs when the dog is left alone, or when the owner merely takes his or her attention off the pet while at home. It is as if the dog were using pica to gain attention, even in the form of punishment.

Note: When a dog swallows something that may be harmful, it is often fed bread or cake to ease the item through his intestines. Another positive reinforcement—food—has thus been given. **The better alternative is to call the veterinarian immediately.**

Corrective Program

From all these causes for pica, you may recognize an element or two common to your situation. Even if not, the following program has solved hundreds of cases and should benefit your dog, if followed strictly.

Most dogs with pica miss their owners too much when left alone or ignored. They strive for all the attention they can get. To make your pet more contented, you will now have to ask that he earn his petting and praise. So each time your dog begs or you want to give him attention, ask him to sit for you. If he is sitting already, ask him to lie down. In other words, get him to function for you.

It is amazing to see dogs settle down and become more relaxed after a few days of this little routine. Avoid prolonged petting; make it only about five seconds. Fondling dogs tends to make them introverted, and pica is a sign of introversion.

Tone Down Emotions

To help your dog stop missing you too much, it will be necessary to defuse the emotions involved in your coming and going from the house.

Before leaving home, take just five minutes and sit down in the area the dog will occupy in your absence. Ignore the dog, read a paper, or just gather your thoughts about the day's activities. This sets a calm, unconcerned prelude to the departure. Do not even make eye contact with the dog. Then get up and leave without any words or ceremony.

At homecoming, say, "Hi," and then go about doing some other business for five minutes. Then you may ask the dog to sit and give him a nice "Hello." However, do this in an area away from the door by which you entered. This avoids too much emotion in the area of your homecoming.

All of these steps will help eliminate the causes for the tension that result in pica. When we get rid of the causes by getting the pet to function for praise and petting, and relieve the emotional uproar about homecomings and goings, the dog should become noticeably more relaxed within a few days or weeks.

After the Fact

What should you do if you come home and the dog has swallowed something? It is too late to take remedial action. The dog has long since forgotten the act of swallowing the article. However, *if you think something harmful has been swallowed, call your veterinarian with-*
out delay.

When you are home and the dog shows interest in something he may swallow, or even if he mouths or chews, distract him instantly. Clap your hands, or slap a wall with your hand or a newspaper. Do not slap the dog or speak to him, because you want to depersonalize the correction so it will be effective even when you are not at home. Then toss a ball or some acceptable chewy toy to provide a substitute for the forbidden article.

Never pick up things while the dog is watching you that you do not want your pet to have. You can actually heighten the desire for it. Dogs seem to enjoy "handling" with their mouths the things we handle.

Play Relaxes

The final element of the program is play. This is especially important if your pet is alone a great deal. Toss a ball or run around and let the dog chase you, at least once a day. Do it in the morning if you can. This helps give proper exercise and also provides an intense, happy emotional interaction that relaxes the dog.

Continue the program at least six weeks. You will not be spending any extra time, only changing the way you are spending time with your pet. The largest sacrifice you will make is emotional–giving up those joyous homecoming celebrations and fondling. However, pica is a serious problem, and the ultimate good for you and your pet is well worth the effort. If your dog is on medical treatment during the program, follow your veterinarian's advice strictly.

Total correction of any behavior problem depends upon the physical well-being of the dog, as well as on his emotional health.

Sympathy Lameness

Nothing is more pitiful than an injured animal, especially a puppy. When it is our own pet, the effect on us can be more upsetting than the injury is to the animal. Sympathy lameness is a condition that occurs long after the animal's injury has healed. A full understanding of the cause brings about the insights needed for a correction.

Causes

Reflexive Paw-Raising

When puppies or older dogs feel concerned about some of life's situations, they often lift one of their forepaws. Some even whine. This behavior stems from early experience with their canine mothers that, after feeding them, nuzzled them over onto their backs and commenced to lick them, first around the muzzle and neck, then down their abdomen and across their genitals and anus. This stimulated their primary reflex to eliminate (urinate and defecate) which is thus a learned reflex in puppies, not a natural reflex as in human and primate infants. During the licking, especially around their muzzles, the still-sightless pups raise their forepaws in an effort to ward off this postfeeding maternal "treatment." The result of all this is that paw-raising is associated with objection to being dominated.

When puppies graduate into the human family, you will often see this behavior come with them. If you roll a pup onto his back and gently hold him immobile, you can usually see the paws start rising immediately. If you hold him thus for thirty seconds or so, you can even judge just how submissive or dominant the pup feels; if he calms down quickly and becomes still, he is fairly submissive; if he struggles fiercely the entire time, he feels fairly or extremely dominant. Submissive pups often raise their paws or even roll onto their backs when scolded. Dominant types often put their paws onto the arms of a person who tries to pet them on the throat and chest.

If you get the idea that submissive types are more prone to sympathy lameness than dominant types, you are on the right track. But it does not always hold true, especially if the lameness starts following a painful experience.

Acquired Sympathy Lameness

There are several ways to cause sympathy lameness. One of the less common is to deliberately teach him. Every time the pup or dog raises his paw, give him a reward, such as sympathetic attention to that paw. Soon each time the pet wants some attention, he will raise the paw.

Accidentally causing the condition is more common and usually follows some incident such as stepping on the paw. This brings about the familiar yip, followed by apologies and cuddling by the remorseful pain inflictor. The pain of the accident was real, but the emotional, apologetic person is telling the pup that this experience is horrible, and warrants a great deal of attention and sympathy. Depending on the sensitivity of the puppy, the degree of pain, and the intensity of the sympathy offered, sympathy lameness may occur later in several circumstances:

- When the puppy or dog wants attention

- When the owner uses a sympathetic tone of voice

- When the paw or limb is handled with concern.

The latter two reasons are easy to relate to the problem. However, the first reason pops up in rather baffling ways.

An unusual case involved a spayed Doberman that had received extreme sympathy as a puppy when he suffered what appeared to be a mild seizure. Thereafter, whenever visitors arrived and his owner's attentions were directed elsewhere, he became hostile toward the guests. On the other hand, when family members gathered to play games, the Doberman would often fall on his side and have another seizure. This interrupted the games, of course, and led to the attention he had learned to attain through what is called pseudoepilepsy.

Another dog may not have a general seizure, but the telltale paw will rise or limping will start in the affected limb.

Many of my cases have involved sympathy lameness in the following situations:

- A new baby arrives home

- A new pet is introduced into the home

- One of the family goes away for some time

- An argument occurs in the home

- There is a general undertone of stress in the emotional environment, such as someone is ill or upset and the dog, in his uncanny way, senses it.

Our pets are incredibly sensitive to our emotions, even when we try to hide them. Therefore, since "feelings" are the key to causing sympathy lameness, they are also the tools for correcting the problem.

Corrective Program

There are two ways to correct sympathy lameness. The first is often the easiest: Avoid the things that bring on the problem. This is simple to do if the lameness only occurs when you use a concerned tone of voice, scold or punish your pet. However, when the various triggers for the lameness are not controllable, a different routine must be used. The dog must be taken through the situations that cause lameness, and then you must show him a different interpretation and a new way to behave instead of becoming lame.

The Jolly Routine

Whenever your dog shows signs of becoming lame, you must start an upbeat, happy activity for everyone, especially the pet. This might be bouncing a ball, running about and tossing a favorite toy, getting the leash and suggesting a quick walk—the Jolly Routine. The routine must be started before the actual lameness sets in and should last three minutes or longer. Then return to whatever activity started the signs of lameness, again switching to the Jolly Routine if there is the slightest sign that the dog is going to act lame again.

At first, you and others in the household may feel a little silly, jumping about joyfully when the dog is asking for sympathy, but switching the pet's mood for concern to one of happy activity will work wonders if you are all sincere and stick to the program.

Repeat the routine until your pet no longer responds with lameness. Undertake this procedure daily if possible, but at least three times weekly until, when you start the activity that formerly produced lameness, you now see the dog get active. When this point is attained, you no longer need to go into your Jolly Routine. However, watch for backsliding. Depending on the age of your pet, it might occur. If it does, restart the routine and cease when the correction is effective.

Take him for a happy-type walk on the leash.

C H A P T E R 3 4

Unruliness

Frustration, embarrassment, and more frustration: These are the emotions dog owners can feel when a pet continually dashes outdoors, or "sexes" visitors by sniffing them in private places. The dog that is just plain overactive, especially when guests arrive, can also be helped toward better behavior with this program. Correction for all these conditions starts with the same step—establishing yourself and other household members as leaders and teachers for the pet.

Corrective Program

Bossy Dogs

If a dog must do something to earn his praise and petting, he soon learns to look to you for guidance in all of life's situations. It is not necessary to break a pet's spirit through punishment or scolding in order to gain control. Rather, consistency and good-natured perseverance are effective and humane. Your understanding and use of the dog's natural language—body movement and stances—also are necessary to leadership.

The following steps are for all household members. Each time your dog asks for attention, ask him to sit. The technique does not require heavy handling. You merely keep your left side toward the dog, lean slightly backward, and bring your right hand through his line of vision to a point above the animal's head. This causes the dog to look upward and back, tracking your hand. Raising his head is the first part of sitting for dogs, so say, "Good sit," when it happens. Keep up this procedure until the dog actually sits. Then praise more and pet him, preferably on the throat and chest. After a few sessions of this over a period of two to four days, the dog should be sitting readily on your spoken sit, or even with the hand movement alone.

Be sure everyone follows this routine with your pet. Use it whenever you want to pet him and when the dog wants your attention.

Some bossy dogs may pout when they realize you are turning the tables on them, that is, asking them to earn their praise and taking a position of leadership with them. Such pouting may include going away from you rather than sitting for you. If this happens, simply go on about your business and ignore the dog. Pouting is great self-therapy for bossy dogs. You will notice that the pet's need for attention overcomes the bossiness, and he will return to sit for praise. This may take up to four days with extremely bossy dogs. It is well worth it, though, since the problems to be worked out will require your leadership.

Dashing Outdoors

Many people like to use the sit to stop a dog from dashing through a door. The trouble with this is twofold. If you forget to ask for the sit, the dog dashes, plus the dog never develops self-control about dashing.

The goal of our method, and it is extremely effective, is to instill self-control over door-dashing in your dog. When this is achieved, a genuine correction has been gained. Therefore, movement and body language will speak more clearly than sit, since these are the natural channels of canine communication.

Learning to use movement with your dog requires that you *react quickly* to the pet. This means you must keep an eye on the dog at all times, being ready to reverse your direction the instant the dog starts to move the wrong way. Here is how it works at the door.

Start to move toward the door through which the dog likes to dash. This might be any door in the house, or only the front door. As you start toward the door, if the dog appears about to go toward it, abruptly back away from the door, praising the dog, even crouching down to attract him away from the portal. During the early part of the program, back up at least five feet from the door. Repeat this until you can approach the door while your dog stays away from it. At this point return quickly to your dog and praise him again.

Phase two involves starting to open the door. As you do so, watch the dog! If he starts to break toward you, repeat the abrupt back-away routine. If you got the door open before your pet moves toward you, slam the door before backing away again to praise him. Repeat this until you can open the door with the dog remaining away. Then, once again, close the door and go back and praise the dog.

Phase three requires you to go through the door, keeping your eye on the dog, and close the door behind you. Stay outside for about thirty seconds. Then go inside to the spot away from the door and praise your dog. At this point you may have to start over at phase one because your dog tends to learn by phases before he can learn the entire procedure as a single process. However, if you will keep repeating the process, the dog will learn it within a few minutes.

Practice this routine on all doors and with all household members. Do it in groups of people as well. Do it with packages in your arms and in all of the situations the dog will encounter in life at the door.

Another interesting technique that works well with dogs that dash merely to be with people is to let the animal go out through the door (into an area safe from any harm, of course). Close the door and leave the dog on the other side. Then open the door and let the pet in or out, as the case may be. Do this a few times and the dog soon will look to you before dashing. However, you must then revert to phase one for long-term correction.

Embarrassing Sniffing or Licking

It does not require an elaborate description to communicate the embarrassment of an owner or the chagrin of a victim when a dog nuzzles the private area of a guest. Even other dogs seem to object to such intrusions. The offending pet, obeying basic, primitive drives, may be curious as to the sex of visitors, but must learn better manners for his own and the owner's long-range well-being. If your pet is among the oversniffers, or licks people to excess, this program is simple and effective.

The dog that learns to sit for his introduction to guests is not only well-mannered but also unoffensive. That is to say, people who may be wary of meeting new dogs seem reassured by a sitting dog. Therefore, *teach your pet to sit and to stay sitting until you release him* by saying "Free." Gradually increase the sitting time from ten seconds to two minutes.

When greeting guests, have the pet sit and then allow the new-comers to say "Hello," offering a hand, palm up, for the dog to sniff. In the event your visitors are confident with dogs, have them crouch down so the pet can scent their breath. To many mammals the essence of our being, in terms of identification, seems to be embodied in our breath. Once they have sampled it, they usually are satisfied and further curiosity is quelled.

Following the hand-and breath-sniff routine, have the guests be seated and release the dog. He may proceed to make the rounds, say-ing another "Hello," and then should calm down.

If the foregoing program is put into effect for a few visits, you should notice your pet sitting automatically when greeting newcom-ers. This is a goal achieved by more than half of the dogs put through this program. If your guests will be staying for longer than an evening, it is best to have them ask the dog to sit for them, then pet and release the dog. This places the guests in a position of control and has proven positive in controlling the sniffer-licker. The entire routine seems to satisfy the pet's basic desire to identify by scent, and the tendency to be curious about parts of the anatomy usually fades in two to six weeks.

The foregoing program should be applied in the very same way for dogs who get overexcited and hyperactive when guests arrive. If it is applied persistently and consistently, the result can be a well-man-nered dog that will be welcome in the house with your guests.

Wetting Submissively

When a puppy or mature dog starts wetting for no reason except that he is approaching or being approached by a person or another dog, or even when entering a certain area, the dog is not urinating deliberately. That is, he is not consciously performing the act but is responding on a purely emotional level. Something about the situation stimulates extreme feelings of submission in the dog.

So that we can understand the dog's point of view in what seems like senseless behavior, let us examine where the act of submissive wetting originates.

Behavioral Causes

The earliest submissive behavior that puppies display is seen after their mother first feeds them. She nudges each pup over onto his back or side with her nose, holds him there and licks him from face to tail. The pup's reaction to this is to raise his paw when the mother is licking his chin and neck, which is where submissive paw raising seems to originate. He then proceeds to urinate and defecate when the mother has licked his genitals and anus, which is where submissive urination has its roots.

As the pup grows older, gaining his eyesight, the mother merely has to look as if she intends to roll him over for the toilet ritual to achieve urination, if not defecation. This saves the mother time and also prepares the pups to become den-trained when they are able to follow the mother outside for their eliminations later in life.

In its early stages, submissive urination is the puppy's response to a dominant look, but as the pups become more mature they gain some control over this response. Depending on experience, it may never again be displayed in adulthood. However, in cases of extreme stress (from the pup's point of view) submissive urination can recur.

One thing is apparent: your submissive wetting pup or dog is probably not deliberately misbehaving, but is responding to excitement, apprehension, or fear. If you understand this, you can deal with the problem without getting angry or upset. Handling submissive wetting problems demands well-controlled emotions if the behavior is to be corrected.

Analyze the Problem

The problem usually occurs when the pet is faced by someone who approaches, takes a stance, looks or speaks threateningly, or elicits excitement, such as at homecomings. Do a little fact finding about your situation to determine when the wetting takes place:

- When you or others are facing the dog?

- When you lean over him?

- When reaching to pick him up?

- When you scold or raise your voice?

- When you or others get excited?

- At homecoming?

If you identify the things that trigger the dog's urination and are prepared to change your behavior, the problem can be cleared up. The time required will be from a few days to up to six weeks, depending on your skill and the severity of the problem.

Corrective Program

The first step is to **remove any signs of threat** at those key times when the dog wets: homecomings, visitors calling, when you scold the dog, and so forth.

- If your pet wets when you approach, do not approach. Instead crouch down and turn your side toward the dog.

- Do not hold out your hand, especially palm down or over the dog's head.

- Avoid direct eye contact.

- Let the dog approach you. If he seems to be under control, pet him lightly under the chin. If this produces wetting, withhold petting for a few more days and then try it again.

Avoid Talking

Avoid speaking at these times for about four days. Then, see if saying "Good dog" will produce wetting. If not, keep up the routine for four days and on these occasions ask the dog to sit and tell him "Good dog" when he complies. If speaking stimulates the wetting, withhold it for four days and then try it again.

Run through the situations at least three times in a row daily if you can. For instance, if entering at homecoming produces it, follow the program as just described, then go out and come in immediately again, and again.

In most situations four days are required before submissive wetting disappears when you remain crouched. When this happens, you should approach the situation standing, keeping sideways to the dog.

If wetting occurs, go back into the crouch. Let the dog's reaction tell you how to behave. If you see that telltale squat begin, back off a step and start over until you can again proceed.

During the program your dog may gain so much confidence that he jumps up on you or others. Tolerate this for a while, say about a week, then just sidestep, and the jumping will usually cease.

Involve Others

Avoid the mistake of carrying out the entire program yourself. Get others into the act. Make sure you let them know the techniques

you are using. Show them. When several other people have gone
through it with the dog, it will help make the correction permanent.

When two weeks have passed with none of the wetting, you can
feel you have reached your goal. In case of backsliding, simply start
at the beginning of the program again. Correction should only take a
few sessions.

Throughout your program be patient, understanding, and optimistic. Your mood will be sensed by your pet, and things will proceed
more quickly.

Whining

The piercing whine of a puppy or an adult dog signals some kind of discomfort, either physical or emotional. Whichever it may be, the sound is extremely grating on human ears. The cause may be loneliness, hunger, cold, or frustration, as in the case of a dog that does not get his own way.

Understanding the Causes

The puppy that whines when left alone is behaving normally during this first experience. If the whining brings about the appearance of people, even if they punish, the odds are strong that the whining will be repeated. After all, puppies are social creatures, raised within litters, so even if a bit unpleasant, having company is often better than feeling totally marooned. If you must isolate your pet, do not make the error of "rescuing" him by punishment or you risk reinforcing the whining behavior.

Emotion is the most important element in the relationship between people and dogs. Therefore, if you satisfy the social (and emotional) needs of your pet, the chances are good that the frustrations which formerly drove him to misbehavior will be relieved and better behavior will result.

Establish Your Leadership

The pet dog that does not feel the need to get his own way is a happier, better adjusted dog than one who thinks he should be the leader over his people. To fill the role of leader, every dog owner needs to exercise the needed principles daily, from moment to moment. It is a mistake to think that several minutes of training per day fulfills this need. It helps, but unless the training dovetails with a total environmental leadership role played by the dog's owners, more harm than good may actually occur. This is due to the dog's extreme sensitivity to inconsistent treatment.

If the owners spoil the dog as a matter of daily practice, but demand obedience in a fifteen to forty-five-minute training session, it is no wonder the animal balks and is even resentful when faced with such "Jekyll and Hyde" personalities. Therefore, the best principle is consistency.

Is your dog an isolation whiner? Or does he start his vocal calisthenics when he does not get his way? Either way, the treatment that succeeds requires the pet to learn to earn his praise and petting from all those living with him. It is useless for one family member to assume the "heavy" role, practicing leadership principles, while everyone else spoils the animal. More confusion results, once again due to inconsistency.

Corrective Program

Teaching to Earn Attention

The principle is easy to recite but requires extreme self-control to practice. Each time the dog asks for attention, or anyone feels like petting him, some function must be performed by the dog. For instance, if the dog approaches and nudges a hand for some petting, the person must, very pleasantly, ask the pet to sit, and then praise and pet him, but only for three to five seconds.

All prolonged petting (fondling) must be stopped for your program to succeed. This practice must be adopted by everyone. Within one to four days you should witness a pet that is more relaxed, actually anxious to please and less likely to get upset when denied something he wants.

Some ultra spoiled dogs withdraw from social contact when the full impact of this program is first appreciated. They actually pout. If this occurs, just let it happen. *Do not press your desires or attentions on the pet.* Pouting is great self-therapy. In a couple of days the dog will be back, asking for his rewards of praise and petting. Then the program may be launched fully.

The earn-your-praise-and-petting principle should be practiced at least six weeks, and preferably for the life of your dog.

Defuse Emotion

If whining occurs only when the pup or dog is isolated, avoid such isolation if possible. If you cannot avoid it, then be sure not to make a fuss over the pet when you put him away or release him from isolation.

For instance, if the dog whines when left in the car, defuse all emotion when you get out of the car. If the dog becomes excited when you return, just ignore him. This is not simple because we all feel flattered that our pets would miss us so. Therefore, we perceive some social obligation to acknowledge the dog's uproarious greetings. Not so. Overemotionalism created the problem, so the correction requires non-emotionalism.

The same procedure should be used wherever the dog does his whining at home, inside or out. Coupled with the overall environmental program, this routine will bring success in from four days to six weeks.

Car Whiners

Some dogs whine intolerably during car rides. Once again, the leader-type animal is the basis for the problem. He cannot control the course of events (drive the car), so he builds tensions due to this frustration, then relieves (or at least tries to relieve) the tension through whining.

If you have this problem, the help offered by the general environmental learn-to-earn portion of the program should be appreciated. Nothing is more exasperating than trying to cope with a car-whiner. However, there is one aid I have found helpful—ear muffs or plugs. These allow some peace of mind for the driver and passengers and make it more bearable to ignore the whining, or to seem to ignore it.

The worst thing to do with a car-whiner is to stop the vehicle. Stopping is just what the dog is ordering, next to getting out of the auto, which is his ultimate desire. So just muff up and bear it! When used together with the general program, you should succeed in a few days to weeks.

During every aspect of the program, keep calm, display good natured optimism and you will wind up with a pet that is a pleasure to be around.

NOTE: If your dog whines only when he lies down, gets up, or otherwise moves about or even when still, consult your veterinarian before instituting any correction. If there is some genuine physical discomfort involved, such as hip dysplasia or intestinal parasites, medical attention is the first step.

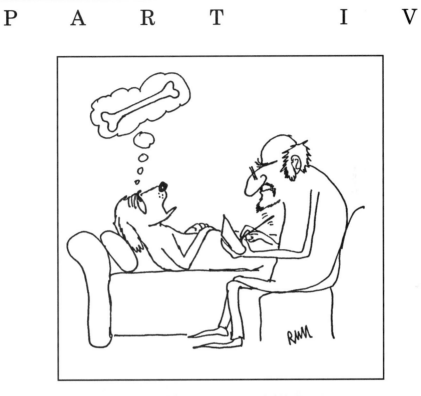

WHEN YOU NEED MORE HELP

C H A P T E R   3 7

Selecting a Behavior Consultant

Sometimes an animal's behavior problems seem so involved that they defy our ability to see them objectively, which is when the services of a behavior consultant can be invaluable. The following guide will help ensure that you select someone who will work with you in a way that allows you to gain the insight needed to correct the problem. The little extra time required is well worth spending, compared to the risks of choosing someone based on the size of their Yellow Pages ad or the appeal of their titles.

The Selection Process

Have Your Pet Examined

Take your problem pet to your veterinarian for a complete physical examination. Take along a fresh stool sample for a parasite check. My records of more than 2,000 cases show that more than 20 percent of dogs with behavior problems that had not been checked in more than six months also had a health problem. There is no use wasting money on a behavior problem when there may be a contributing health factor.

Get at Least Two Referrals

After the physical examination, ask the doctor about the behavior problem and whether you might benefit from professional consultation. If the answer is yes and consultants are recommended, make notes about each specialist and ask what sort of feedback has been received from other clients so referred. If any of those clients are acquaintances of yours, talk to them before telephoning any specialists on the list.

Many veterinarians themselves are getting involved in consulting about problems, so if your pet's doctor has some ideas, listen to them. If they sound reasonable and appealing, you might be well advised to follow the veterinarian's suggestions before contacting anyone else. But, give the advice time to work and follow the instructions carefully.

Qualifying the Consultants

The telephone call to the specialist is aimed at gathering vital information about how he or she goes about working with owners and their problem pets. But keep in mind, just as you are qualifying them, they are also qualifying you! If they are operating on the highest ethical standards, they will want to know a great deal about you, your pet and his health history, plus the history of the problem from the beginning to the present time. They should be especially interested in what steps you may have already taken to solve the problem yourself or with other assistance. Give them all the facts. This will allow them to decide if they can really help, or if they should refer you to someone more specialized in the problem.

On the other hand, if they show no interest in the history of the problem and simply press you for an appointment, count your blessings, thank them nicely, hang up and contact the next consultant on the list. Anyone in this profession who does not extend the courtesy of qualifying his or her clients through a few minutes on the telephone falls into one or more of the following categories:

- They lack the necessary experience and/or training to do it. Why pay them to educate themselves on your animal?

- They subscribe to the new car dealer's "system house" approach, which states: "You can't get their check and close a deal on the phone." This is not very professional.

- They are too acutely dog-oriented to appreciate your role in the problem, especially if they use the old story that they must "see" your pet before anything can be decided.

- They are too "science" centered to develop a genuine feeling for your problem.

Any of the above types display a lack of understanding about the emotional state of someone sincerely seeking help for a pet. They fail to respond as a well-trained consultant should respond, which is with empathy. Add this to the fact that they do not qualify their clients in order to save time, effort, and money for all concerned.

Get the Facts and Understand Them

If the specialist offers a description of the programs available, listen carefully and make notes. Be sure all of the following questions are answered to your satisfaction. While you are gathering this information, don't hesitate to interrupt to ask for an explanation of any term or procedure you do not understand.

Questions to Ask

- Where and how long will the appointments be? Sixty to ninety minutes is usual for appointments.

- Who must attend? Make sure everyone involved in the problem and correction procedures can attend.

- What will we be doing? Get "operational descriptions," such as sitting and talking, training the dog, and so on.

- How many appointments will be required? Six weekly meetings usually suffice, even for severe problems.

- Will any special equipment be required? If so, what? This will reveal whether or not shock collars, spike collars, hanging nooses, hobbles, ultrasonic devices, etc. will be used. If so, get descriptions of how they will be used.

- What is the most severe physical treatment that may be required? This lets you know if ear-biting, kneeing, kicking, hitting, jerking, or shaking are part of the program.

- If the problem persists after the program is completed, what happens? This will prepare you for further meetings and/or charges if things do not go as expected.

- How much will it cost?

With these questions answered, you can qualify the specialist on three accounts:

1. The humaneness of the methods to be employed, which is up to your own personal tastes.

2. The cost of the program in terms of the money, time, and effort you will be investing.

3. What sort of rapport you and the specialist establish. If you and the consultant cannot communicate smoothly during an explanation of the programs, you're apt to have even more difficulty later when it comes to understanding the causes and corrections for your pet's problem.

When you have satisfied yourself that you have reached the "right" specialist, your chances for success are almost as good as they can possibly be. However, after thirty-one years of consultation work with dog owners, I would be failing you (and my conscience) if I didn't mention a few more precautions.

There are some impressive "silver tongues" in this field. They are exceptionally good at using the telephone interview to gain a pet owner's confidence and a preliminary meeting. To avoid getting involved in something that may not be satisfactory for you or your pet, hark back to the consultant's description of the actual programs and watch out for the following:

- Beware of anyone who says that they can "do it for you." Ask them to meet you at the local lake or river and see if they also walk on water. If they can, check for barely submerged rocks.

- Watch out for anyone who says you will be meeting with their "assistant," and that they (the specialist) will supervise.

- Watch out for people who lead you to believe the program is going to be easy. Solving a pet behavior problem is rarely simple. It requires your mental effort and often some emotional adjustments on the part of all family members.

- Watch out for someone who tries to make you feel guilty about your pet's problem. The problem is the result of interactions between your pet and his people, plus other elements in our environment. Anything you have done that helped create the problem was done without harmful intent. No guilt feelings are warranted, only a resolve to eliminate the problem.

C H A P T E R 3 8

Obedience Training

A Family Affair

Everyone ought to go to an enlightened dog obedience class. Puppy classes can be particularly enriching, but check with your veterinarian regarding possible health restrictions. Please note, I said "everyone" ought to go, meaning the whole family. In this way, your dog will quickly learn to respond to all his people uniformly.

More and more obedience instructors are abandoning the old "one-dog, one-trainer" concept.

Full family participation can help you avoid problems. One family member handles the dog in class, but everyone attends and participates in homework exercises between classes. As a result, everyone gains leash control of the dog, not just the person who takes him to class. Also, if another family member is having special problems at home, the instructor can usually assist him or her effectively during or after class.

Finding the Instructor

Ask your veterinarian to refer an instructor. To avoid possible disappointment after enrolling in a class, telephone and ask the following questions:

- Will anyone other than me or my family actually handle my dog?

- Do you ever recommend hanging or swinging a dog on his leash as a correction?

- Do you recommend or use pain to correct unwanted behavior?

A "yes" answer to any of these indicates that you may experience, or witness, training techniques that cause many people to drop out of obedience classes. Another major reason people quit is a lack of sufficient personal attention to special problems. So it is a good idea to find out if the instructor makes time available for such things. If not, you are probably better off looking elsewhere.

Prepare for Class

You can make obedience class a delightful experience for everyone, including your dog, if you will prepare for class. At least a week before the first meeting put the dog on the earned praise and petting program. Have everyone in the family tell him to sit before petting and praise. This is to be done every time the dog seeks attention or affection. Then, make the petting and praise brief. Release him from the sit by saying "Free" after a few seconds. During the week, two or three times a day, stand with the dog at your left side, tell him to sit, and gradually extend the time of the sit until he will stay still for two minutes.

This simple exercise will give you a valuable head start on life in obedience class, where you will be expected to hold your dog's attention in spite of distractions of other dogs and people.

Helpful Reading

Campbell, W. E.: *Behavior Problems in Dogs*. Moseby Yearbook Publications, Santa Barbara, 1975.

Mery, F.: *The Life, History and Magic of the Dog.* Grossett & Dunlop, New York, 1970.

Scott, J. P. and Fuller, J. L.: *Dog Behavior: The Genetic Basis*. University of Chicago Press, 1965.

Shah, I.: *The Sufis*. Doubleday, New York, 1962.

Tuttle, J. L., editor: *Dogs Need Our Love*. Libra, Roslyn Heights, NY, 1983.

Index

About the Author

Bill Campbell's early, post-high school education and work was in television and radio writing and broadcasting. He then trained in industrial psychology in England and designed and conducted employee motivational courses for an international firm.

In 1967, after declaring independence from corporate life, he studied and worked with Dare Miller, Ph.D., at the Canine Behavior Center in Los Angeles. In 1971 he and Peggy established the Dog Owner Guidance Service at their one-acre ranch in the San Fernando Valley. His dog behavior case histories and articles were published in *Modern Veterinary Practice* during the 1970s when he served as contributing editor on canine behavior. The first edition of *Behavior Problems in Dogs* was published in 1975. He was a founding member of the American Society of Veterinary Ethology, and is an affiliate member of its succeeding organization, the American Veterinary Society of Veterinary Behavior.

Bill and wife Peggy now reside in Grants Pass, Oregon, where they publish and market the *Pet Behavior Newsletter*, the *BehavioRx* client education series of problem correction brochures, available from many veterinary clinics and hospitals. Bill was recently appointed to *Dog Fancy* magazine's Hall of Fame and continues to lecture and conduct seminars for pet professionals.

About the Illustrator

Dr. Bob Miller (RMM) cartooned his way through the Colorado State University School of Veterinary Medicine, graduating in 1956. He has practiced in Thousand Oaks, California, ever since, where his daily practice experiences serve as inspiration for his cartoons and writing. American Veterinary Publications (Santa Barbara, CA) has published five books of his cartoons and comic verse. His cartoons have appeared regularly in *Modern Veterinary Practice* and other magazines, and he writes a monthly column for *Veterinary Medicine*. In 1985 his autobiographical book, *Most of My Patients are Animals* (Paul S. Ericksson, Middlebury, VT) was published, with an introduction by his friend and colleague, James Herriot.

For Information on Sof-Touch™ Leashes

BehavioR$_X$ Systems
P. O. Box 1658
Grants Pass, OR 97528

or

Visit the Pet Behavior Resources website

www.webtrail.com/petbehavior

Additional Alpine Titles of Interest

How to Raise a Puppy You Can Live With
Clarice Rutherford and David H. Neil, MRCVS
This book is the "puppy owner's Dr. Spock,"— a cookbook approach as to what to do at what age to socialize your puppy and bring him up as a respectable member of society. Use it in conjunction with this book, or to help select and start your next puppy.

Successful Obedience Handling
Barbara Handler
This book will help you sharpen your performance in the obedience ring. It works with any training method, and is guaranteed to improve your scores. Not a training manual — this book is for the competitive obedience handler.

Love on A Leash, Giving Joy Through Pet Therapy
Liz Palika
Now that you have a perfectly behaved dog, take him out and let the rest of the world enjoy him! Learn how to train your dog for nursing home and children's home visits, hospital visitation, and more. Put your behavior training to work and reap the rewards—the joy of giving something back to society.

Coping with Sorrow on the Loss of Your Pet
Moira Anderson Allen
If you or a friend has just lost a faithful companion, this book will help you through the grief. You'll learn about the choices available for burial, how to help your children through the ordeal, and when it's time to get a new pet. There's a chapter on finding a lost pet, too.

For a Free Catalog
of other Alpine titles

Call 1-800-777-7257

Learn more about us on our website:
www.alpinepub.com

800 434-1211